To C.
our neighbor
in U.S.A.
Rich blessings
to you.

Nils Olav

2017 July

NOW CONCERNING
SPIRITUAL GIFTS
I WOULD NOT HAVE YOU IGNORANT

Use of the following studies on the Baptism and Gifts of the Holy Spirit is encouraged for the edification of the Body of the Lord Jesus Christ.

Nils Olson
Missionary/Pastor/Teacher
Munakata Bethel Christian Center (Japan)
January, 1982 ~ November, 2016

NOW CONCERNING SPIRITUAL GIFTS
I Would Not Have You Ignorant

2017 Nils Olson

Unless otherwise noted, Scripture quotations are taken from the Authorized King James Version.

ISBN-13: 978-1548257194

ISBN-10: 1548257192

Printed in USA
Cover design by James Xavier

CONTENTS

7	Preface
11	Introduction
19	Now concerning BAPTISM OF THE HOLY SPIRIT
20	Purposes of the Holy Spirit Baptism
25	How to receive the Baptism of the Holy Spirit
31	This Side or That Side of The Needle
33	Now concerning GIFTS OF GOD
41	Now concerning GIFTS OF THE HOLY SPIRIT
43	UTTERANCE GIFT-Prophecy
46	UTTERANCE GIFT-Tongues
52	UTTERANCE GIFT-Interpretation of Tongues
57	POWER GIFT-Faith
61	POWER GIFT-Working of Miracles
71	POWER GIFT-Gift(s) of Healing(s)
81	REVELATION GIFT-The Word of Wisdom
86	REVELATION GIFT-The Word of Knowledge
97	REVELATION GIFT-The Discerning of Spirits
113	The Last Word
115	Author Profile

Preface

In teaching this material on the Holy Spirit's gifts, it will be helpful to explain to those being taught what you, as a believer in the Body of Christ, have experienced in being used by the Holy Spirit in His gifts. For example, if the Holy Spirit has used, or is using you to give messages in tongues, interpreting, prophecy, words of wisdom, knowledge, gifts of healings, faith, working of miracles and discerning spirits, how does He prepare your heart to minister the gift? It may be the first time many of you have ever heard about these wonderful gifts. Teaching you what to expect can and will dispel any fear you may have about operating in the gifts. The student only knows and can practice what he has been taught; and they say, "experience is the best teacher."

If you have not been used in any of the gifts of the Holy Spirit, and have no "experience" to tell about, open up the subject and ask others to share how they have been used, what they experienced when the Holy Spirit is about to use them.

Years ago, we never spoke about being used by the Holy Spirit to minister a gift for FEAR that pride would grip us and take control. Many times the Holy Spirit cannot operate His gifts through people because of fear. Fear kills faith, and faith is necessary to operate in the gifts of the Holy Spirit. However, such a great desire to see those in the local Body of Christ being used by the Holy Spirit has welled-up in us, that we realize people will never learn unless they are taught.

New Christians and old ones alike have many questions about these necessary gifts of the Spirit. It seems that it is expected that the "Pentecostal" Christian should already know all about them. NOT SO! Some "Pentecostal" churches do not even instruct their people in this important subject, nor are there any manifestations of the Holy Spirit's gifts in their times of gathering together to worship the Lord.

In that Paul wrote to the Corinthian church, *"Now concerning*

I Would Not Have You Ignorant

spiritual gifts, brethren, I would not have you ignorant," there was obviously a lack of knowledge and teaching in the early church regarding the nine gifts of the Holy Spirit. I believe the same lack is evident in the Church today. Hosea prophesied, *My people are destroyed for lack of knowledge . . .* It is my hope this book will help you become more knowledgeable to the wonderful Holy Spirit and the gifts with which He desires to bless the Church.

If your heart is open and sincere to learn about these gifts, as well as the moving of the Holy Spirit in the church world today, then there is no need to worry about the manifestation of the gifts being "wild fire" or "the flesh." There are some who will operate in their own selves, yes, but because you have been given the Holy Spirit, He will witness to your spirit that it is not He.

But ye have an unction (anointing) from the Holy One, and ye know all things . . . but as the same anointing teacheth you of all things, and is truth, and is no lie, and even as it hath taught you, ye shall abide in Him. 1 John 2:20, 27.

This book is written that you may *"grow in the grace and knowledge of our Lord and Savior, Jesus Christ."*

—Nils Olson, June 2017

Appreciation to the following members of the Body of Christ for the use of their notes in this study on the Baptism and Gifts of the Holy Spirit:

HAGIN, Kenneth E.
"Concerning Spiritual Gifts," Kenneth Hagin Ministries, Tulsa, OK 74150, USA. 1974.

HAYES, Norvel
"Seven Ways Jesus Heals," Harrison House, Tulsa, OK 74153, USA. 1982.

IVERSON, Dick
"The Holy Spirit Today," Revised Edition, Bible Temple, Inc., Portland, OR 97213, USA. 1976.

PENTECOST, Dwight
"Your Adversary The Devil," Zondervan Pub., Grand Rapids, MI 49506, USA. 1969.

UNGER, Merrill P.
"Unger's Bible Dictionary," 3rd ed., Moody Bible Institute, Chicago, IL, USA. 1974.

WAGNER, C. Peter
"Your Spiritual Gifts," 3rd printing, Regal Books, G/L Pub., Ventura, CA, USA. 1980.

Introduction
by James H. Feeney

Used by permission © 2017 **www.jimfeeney.org/**

Pastor Jim Feeney, Ph.D., has more than forty years experience in Pentecostal ministry. He has served as a church planter, pastor, and Bible College teacher and Dean in Alaska, New York, and Oregon. Jim has earned his B.A. in English from Boston College, an MBA from Santa Clara University, and a Ph.D. in Church Administration from Trinity Theological Seminary. After 31 years of full-time ministry, he retired in 2006 to devote more time to his family and to building his website.

Why Most Church Services Today Are Powerless

Thousands of American churches have good preaching and uplifting worship of God. But sadly, far fewer have any consistent manifestation of God's power through the supernatural gifts of the Holy Spirit. And that is a major reason why so many church services today seem powerless.

1 Corinthians 14:26 NKJV—*How is it then, brethren? Whenever you* **come together***, each of you has a* **psalm***, has a* **teaching***, has a* **tongue***, has a* **revelation***, has an* **interpretation***. Let all things be done for* **edification***.*

For twenty centuries Christian congregations have gathered to **worship** the Lord ("a psalm") and to hear His **Word** preached and taught ("a teaching"). But what has been **missing** for most of those twenty centuries has been the **gifts of the Holy Spirit**, represented here by "a tongue . . . a revelation . . . an interpretation [of tongues]." The apostle Paul taught that a typical church service, when the believers "come together," would include three elements: (1) worship of the Lord, (2) the Word of God, and (3) the gifts of the Spirit. I liken it to a three-legged stool. As long as all three legs are present, all is well. But if any one of the three legs is missing, the stool becomes very unstable and unable to fulfill its designed purpose.

It's the same in the Lord's Church and the local gathering of the believers. Remove any of the three "legs" (Word, worship, or gifts), and the meeting falls short of the norm for the New Testament church service. What I see in American churches today is generally good (sometimes excellent) worship of God and preaching/teaching of His Word, the Bible. But notably *lacking* in most church services is the manifestation of the spiritual gifts listed in 1 Corinthians 12:8-10 — *the word of wisdom, the word of knowledge, faith, gifts of healing, working of miracles, prophecy, discerning of spirits, divers kinds of tongues, and the interpretation of tongues.*

I know a couple who live in a city whose metropolitan area has well over a quarter million people. They were diligently looking for a good church to attend. But they recently told me that they were having a difficult time (in a city of that size) finding a church that had regular manifestations of the gifts of the Spirit. I was saddened to hear that, but it confirmed my own observations, as well as things I have read about the American church today.

So how, biblically speaking, should Christians solve this widespread lack of the supernatural gifts of the Holy Spirit of God? I suggest three things:

First, believe from God's Word that the gifts of the Holy Spirit *are for today*.

Secondly, believe from God's Word that the churches, as well as God's people individually, *need* the manifestation of the spiritual gifts.

Thirdly, *covet, be zealous for, press in* to be used in the Holy Spirit's gifts.

Believe that the Gifts of the Spirit are for today

1 Corinthians1:5-8 Amplified Bible © 2015 — *... in everything you were* [exceedingly] *enriched in Him, in all speech* **[empowered by the spiritual gifts]** *and in all knowledge* [with insight into the faith].

*In this way our testimony about Christ was confirmed and established in you, so that you are **not lacking in any spiritual gift** [which comes from the Holy Spirit], **as you eagerly wait** [with confident trust] for the revelation of our Lord Jesus Christ **[when He returns]**. And He will also* **confirm you** *to the end* . . .

Verses 7-8 NIV—*Therefore you do **not lack any spiritual gift** as you eagerly wait for our Lord Jesus Christ to be revealed. He will also keep you firm* **to the end** . . .

Verse 7 NLT—*You* **have the gifts of the Holy Spirit** *that you need* **while** *you wait for the Lord Jesus Christ to* **come again**.

The apostle Paul is writing to a local Christian church in Corinth. He expressed gladness that they did "not lack any spiritual gift." Could the apostle write that to *your church* today? This is the same Corinthian church to which Paul wrote about the spiritual gifts in chapter 12. Here at the outset of his epistle, he reminded them that they did **not lack any** of the spiritual gifts. In what time context? — "to the **end** . . . waiting for when **[Christ] returns** . . . **while** [they] wait for the Lord **Jesus to come again**."

The inspired writer Paul expected the local church in Corinth *to have gifts* of the Spirit functioning *throughout the Church Age*, right up until the time of Jesus' Second Coming. And thankfully, there are still thousands of local churches throughout the land today who believe God's Word and see the regular manifestation of the spiritual gifts. But sadly those churches are greatly outnumbered by those which have let the gifts slip from view and from practice, in many cases due to lack of teaching or erroneous teaching on the subject.

Mark 16:15-20 NIV—*[Jesus] said to them, "Go into* **all the world and preach the gospel to all creation** . . . *17 And* **these signs will accompany** *those who believe: In my name they will* **drive out demons***; they will* **speak in new tongues***; 18 they will pick up snakes with their hands; and when they drink deadly poison, it will not hurt them at all; they will place their* **hands on sick people**, **and they will get well** . . . *20 Then the disciples went out and preached everywhere, and the* **Lord worked with them and confirmed his**

I Would Not Have You Ignorant

word by the signs *that accompanied it.*

There are portions of Christ's Great Commission in all four Gospels and in Acts chapter one. Christians almost universally (and correctly) believe that the Great Commission is for the entire Church Age. In Matthew's parallel account (28:18-20), Jesus sent them forth and promised to be with His people "even unto the end of the world." (20) as they went "to all nations" with His Gospel. Mark speaks of Jesus *confirming* the Word with supernatural signs (exorcisms, tongues, and healings) as His followers preached "in *all the world.*"

The Great Commission, along with the accompanying supernatural manifestations of the Spirit, is for "all creation . . . all nations . . . all the world . . . even *unto the end* of the world."

Believe that the Church today needs the spiritual gifts

1 Corinthians 14:12 NASB—*So also you, since you are zealous of* ***spiritual gifts****, seek to* ***abound for the*** <u>***edification***</u> *of the church.*

New American Bible— *. . . seek to have an* ***abundance*** *of them* <u>***for building up***</u> *the church.*

I need edifying, you need edifying, the Lord's churches need to be edified and built up. And one of God's provisions **to build up, to edify** the church is an **abundance of spiritual gifts**. For example:

1 Corinthians 14:24-25 RSV—*If all* ***prophesy****, and an unbeliever or outsider enters [the church service], he* ***is convicted*** *by all, he is called to account by all, the* ***secrets of his heart*** *are disclosed; and so, falling on his face,* ***he will worship God and declare that God is really among you.***

The apostle Paul gives an excellent example of the need for the gifts of the Spirit in the church. Here he speaks of an unbeliever (or outsider) coming into the service and hearing the gift of prophecy. The word of prophecy speaks directly to his heart, brings him under conviction, and leads him to worship God and to acknowledge that God is truly present in the Church.

I saw a similar, remarkable example in a church service in Alaska once. A member of the church was given a revelation through a "word of knowledge" by the Holy Spirit during the Sunday service. He stood and spoke it: "Someone here came to church today needing to be saved. And you know who you are because before coming to church today *you drank two beers*." Astonished by this, a man near the front of the church immediately raised his hand and acknowledged that this word was speaking about him. And he went out with the elders for prayer and asked Jesus to save him and make him a born-again child of God.

A big part of the powerlessness of many church services today is the absence of supernatural gifts from the Holy Spirit. The people sing and worship, then the pastor preaches the Word. And both those things are good and very important. But rarely, if ever, in most churches are there any of the supernatural manifestations of the Holy Spirit. This should not be so! Note the apostle Paul's teaching in the verses just below:

1 Thessalonians 1:5 NASB— . . . our gospel did **not** come to you in **word only**, but **also in <u>power</u> and in the <u>Holy Spirit</u>** . . .

1 Corinthians 2:4-5 NIV—*My message and **my preaching** were not with wise and persuasive words, but **with a demonstration of the Spirit's power**, so that your faith might not rest on human wisdom, but on God's power.*

Do the church and world need Gospel preaching and biblical teaching? Absolutely! But Paul said that the Gospel must come not just in **words**, but "also in **power** and in **the Holy Spirit** . . . with a **<u>demonstration</u>** of the **Spirit's power**." Many of today's churches do indeed have good preaching. But far fewer see that preaching accompanied "with a demonstration of the Spirit's power" through the supernatural gifts of the Spirit. And it is this word-and-power ministry — not "word only," said Paul — that helps hearers place their faith not in human wisdom, but on God's power.

I Would Not Have You Ignorant

Be Zealous for and Eagerly Desire the Gifts of the Spirit

1 Corinthians 14:1, 12, 39 NIV—*Follow the way of love and **eagerly desire** gifts of the Spirit, especially prophecy . . . Since you **are eager for gifts** of the Spirit, **try to excel** in those that build up the church . . . **be eager** prophesy, and do **not forbid** speaking in tongues*.

Frankly, lest we beat around the bush (Paul didn't!), one of the greatest causes of today's powerless churches is their **pastors discouraging or forbidding** the operation of the gifts of the Spirit. The apostolic command in verse 39 is "do *not forbid* speaking in tongues." Paul had just finished giving an inspired teaching on prophecy, tongues, and interpretation. And he concluded that with two key thoughts: (1) "be eager to prophesy" and (2) "do not forbid speaking in tongues." Sadly, in many of today's churches we see the exact opposite: (1) no eagerness to prophesy or to be used in other spiritual gifts, and (2) church leaders compounding the problem by discouraging or even forbidding the public manifestation of the Holy Spirit's gifts.

Our church services today need the same things the Lord placed in the early Church. That is, (1) the ***Word*** of God, (2) ***worship*** of God, and (3) the ***gifts*** of the Holy Spirit. Then and now, that was and is the norm for God's assembled believers, as Paul wrote in our opening verse: 1 Corinthians 14:26 NKJV *How is it then, brethren? Whenever you **come together**, each of you has a **psalm**, has a **teaching**, has a **tongue**, has a **revelation**, has an **interpretation**. Let all things be done for edification.*

When the Corinthian church came together to honor and seek the Lord, they *worshiped* Him ("a psalm"). They preached and taught His *Word*, the Bible ("a teaching." KJV says "a doctrine." And they were blessed and edified by the supernatural manifestation of the *spiritual gifts*, represented here by "a tongue, a revelation, an interpretation."

Any church that does *not worship* the Lord is greatly lacking. Likewise, a church that does not faithfully preach and teach *God's Word* is doing a great disservice to its people. And just as surely, any church failing to make room for the supernatural manifestations/*gifts of the Holy Spirit* is depriving its people of the "demonstration of the Spirit's power" that the apostle Paul wrote was so necessary.

My final word of encouragement to you is that of the inspired apostle in Ephesians 5:18 NIV . . . ***be filled with the Spirit***. Serve Jesus diligently as your Lord and Savior. Also look to Him as the One that all four Gospels reveal as the Baptizer in the the Holy Spirit.

Matthew 3:11 NIV—*I baptize you with water for repentance. But after me comes one who is more powerful than I, whose sandals I am not worthy to carry. He will baptize you with the Holy Spirit and fire.*

Mark 1:8 NIV—*I baptize you with water, but he will baptize you with the Holy Spirit.*

Luke 3:16 NIV—John answered them all, *"I baptize you with water. But one who is more powerful than I will come, the straps of whose sandals I am not worthy to untie. He will baptize you with the Holy Spirit and fire."*

John 1:33-34 NIV—*And I myself did not know him, but the one who sent me to baptize with water told me, 'The man on whom you see the Spirit come down and remain is the one who will baptize with the Holy Spirit.' I have seen and testify that this is God's Chosen One.*

Look to Jesus for the power-giving baptism with the Holy Spirit.

Acts 1:5, 8 NIV—[Jesus said,] *For John baptized with water, but in a few days you will be baptized with the Holy Spirit . . . But you will receive power when the Holy Spirit comes on you; and you will be my witnesses in Jerusalem, and in all Judea and Samaria, and to the ends of the earth.*

And let that supernatural anointing lead you into manifesting one or more of the gifts of the Holy Spirit. If each of us believers does that, it will bring great expression of the power of God to our church services, people will be blessed and edified, and God will be greatly glorified.

—James Feeney

NOW CONCERNING SPIRITUAL GIFTS

I WOULD NOT HAVE YOU IGNORANT

The BAPTISM of The HOLY SPIRIT

*. . . and preached, saying,
There cometh one mightier than I after me, the latchet of
whose shoes I am not worthy to stoop down and unloose.
I indeed have baptized you with water: but he shall
baptize you with the Holy Ghost.* Mark 1:7-8

*He that believeth on me, as the scripture hath said,
out of his belly shall flow rivers of living water.
(But this spake he of the Spirit, which they that
believe on him should receive: for the Holy Ghost
was not yet given; because that Jesus was not
yet glorified.* John 7:38-39

Purposes of the Holy Spirit Baptism

The Greek definition of the word *baptism* (bap-tid-zo) means fully wet. It comes from the root word bap-to and means to cover wholly. Therefore, the Holy Spirit Baptism covers every aspect of the Christian's daily life spiritually, emotionally and physically.

The purpose of the Baptism of The Holy Spirit is manifold (many-folded). The next few paragraphs will list those purposes, scriptural references, and some personal observations.

The Holy Spirit is given to us in order . . .

— **To comfort.** Jesus left and returned to Heaven. The Holy Spirit takes Jesus' place in the life of the believer.

If ye love me, keep my commandments. And I will pray the Father, and he shall give you another Comforter, that he may abide with you for ever; Even the Spirit of truth; whom the world cannot receive, because it seeth him not, neither knoweth him: but ye know him; for he dwelleth with you, and shall be in you. I will not leave you comfortless: I will come to you. John 14:15-18.

— **To teach us the things of God.**

But the Comforter, which is the Holy Ghost, whom the Father will send in my name, he shall teach you all things, and bring all things to your remembrance, whatsoever I have said unto you. John 14:26;

Howbeit when he, the Spirit of truth, is come, he will guide you into all truth: for he shall not speak of himself; but whatsoever he shall hear, that shall he speak: and he will shew you things to come. John 16:13.

— **To write God's Law in our hearts.**

But this shall be the covenant that I will make with the house of Israel; After those days, saith the Lord, I will put my law in their inward parts, and write it in their hearts; and will be their God, and they shall be my people. Jeremiah 31:33.

— **To make us holy, like God.** The HOLY Spirit. "Christian" means "one like Christ," or "Christ-one."

But as he which hath called you is holy, so be ye holy in all manner of conversation; Because it is written, Be ye holy; for I am holy. 1 Peter 1:15-16.

— **To help us preach and teach about Jesus.**

But ye shall receive power, after that the Holy Ghost is come upon you: and ye shall be witnesses unto me both in Jerusalem, and in all Judaea, and in Samaria, and unto the uttermost part of the earth. Acts. 1:8.

Witnesses TESTI-fy. Note that Jesus became anointed first, and then taught with astonishing power.

And they were astonished at his doctrine: for he taught them as one that had authority, and not as the scribes. And they were all amazed, insomuch that they questioned among themselves, saying, What thing is this? what new doctrine is this? for with authority commandeth he even the unclean spirits, and they do obey him. Mark 1:22, 27.

The word "testify" in our English language comes from the Latin root word "testis," which is the singular of "testes," the male reproductive glands. "Testimony" means, therefore, to give evidence, witness with authoritative *dunamis*, power. The ultimate goal of every Christian should be to REPRODUCE one of his own kind! This cannot be done if one is "impotent." Therefore, the "power" (potency, dunamis) of the Holy Ghost is a vital necessity for the Christian.

— **To uplift, encourage, build up the church body and oneself.**

"But the manifestation of the (Holy) Spirit is given to every man to profit withal." 1 Corinthians 12:7

"But ye, beloved, building up yourselves on your most holy faith, praying in the Holy Ghost, keep yourselves in the love of God . . ." Jude 20-21

— To manifest the fruit of God, that is His very personality and character, in our everyday lives.

But the fruit of the Spirit is love, joy, peace, longsuffering, gentleness, goodness, faith, Meekness, temperance: against such there is no law. Galatians 5:22-23.

— To clothe us with God's power and holiness.

(Amplified Bible) *"For as many of you as were baptized into Christ, into a spiritual union and communion with Christ, the Anointed One, the Messiah, have put on, clothed yourselves with Christ."* Galatians 3:27

Ephesians 6:14-18 indicates that it is the Holy Spirit who clothes us with God's armor. *". . . Stand therefore having your loins girt about with truth* (by someone else)*, and having on the breastplate of righteousness; and your feet shod with the preparation of the gospel of peace . . . "*

But we must each individually *"take the shield of faith, the helmet of salvation, and the sword of the Spirit, which is the word of God, and pray in the Spirit."*

We must explain something very important here. We trust that you will not misunderstand, but rather come to the understanding that Jesus is not Christ. "Christ" is not Jesus' last name. Jesus is THE Christ, THE Anointed One, THE Messiah. Christ is the anointing of God, that is, the Holy Ghost. Notice the scriptures below. Parenthetical entries are for your easier understanding.

Acts 17:3
Opening and alleging, that Christ (the MESSIAH) *must needs have suffered, and risen again from the dead; and that this Jesus, whom I preach unto you, is* (the) *Christ* (that is MESSIAH, anointed one).

Acts 18:5
And when Silas and Timotheus were come from Macedonia, Paul was pressed in the spirit, and testified to the Jews that Jesus was (the) *Christ.*

Acts 18:28 *For he mightily convinced the Jews, and that publicly, shewing by the scriptures that Jesus was* (the) *Christ.*

There is a difference between receiving the Holy Spirit at new birth and what we call "the baptism of the Holy Spirit." They are two distinct experiences. Most denominational groups teach from John 20:19-23 that we receive the baptism of the Holy Spirit at conversion. John's description in this portion of Scripture " . . . *he breathed on them, and saith unto them Receive ye the Holy Ghost . . .* " and Paul's description of " . . . *if any man be in Christ, he is a new creature* (creation) . . . " can simply be crossed referenced with the natural creation of Adam in Genesis 2:7, where the LORD God " . . . *formed man of the dust of the ground, and breathed into his nostrils the breath of life; and man became a living soul."*

Paul declares simply in the Amplified of 1 Corinthians 15:45-46 that " . . . *it is not the spiritual life* (breath) *which came first, but the physical and then the spiritual."* The Holy Spirit is the one who births us into the family of God; it is Jesus who breathes on us His breath to give us new life in Christ. But the baptism of the Holy Spirit is another distinct experience.

I Would Not Have You Ignorant

How to receive the Baptism of the Holy Spirit

PIPE — FAUCET — ACTION — WATER

When one is "born again of the Spirit," the Holy Spirit is already residing in the heart of the believer. It is just exactly like water existing in the **pipe** of the kitchen **faucet**. In order to receive the full benefit of that life-giving, satisfying, thirst-quenching water, **YOU must first act** by opening up the faucet to letting the **water** flow out!

Let's say that again — The water is in the pipe, just as the Holy Spirit is already indwelling your innermost being. You simply turn on the faucet, open up your mouth and let the Holy Spirit flow out.

Just as the power of a city's entire water supply is in the pipes of every household, so the power of God's Holy Spirit resides in the

I Would Not Have You Ignorant

believer. Unless a faucet is turned on or opened up, the water remains only in the pipe, but when turned on and allowed to flow out, the water brings refreshing to quench thirst, bring life and cleanse. The same principle applies to the baptism of the Holy Spirit.

Acts 2:37-39 shows us that repentance and water baptism are necessary to receive the baptism of the Holy Spirit. However, it is noted in Acts 10:44-48 their water baptism followed their having received the baptism of the Spirit. If this is the case, it is recommended that water baptism take place as soon afterward as possible.

Acts 2:37-38 *Now when they heard this, they were pricked in their heart, and said unto Peter and to the rest of the apostles, Men and brethren, what shall we do? Then Peter said unto them,* **Repent, and be** *(water)* **baptized** *every one of you in the name of Jesus Christ for the remission of sins, and* **ye shall receive the gift of the Holy Ghost**. *For the promise is unto you, and to your children, and to all that are afar off, even as many as the Lord our God shall call.*

Acts 10:44-48 *While Peter yet spake these words, the Holy Ghost fell on all them which heard the word. And they of the circumcision which believed were astonished, as many as came with Peter, because that on the Gentiles also was poured out the gift of the Holy Ghost. For they heard them speak with tongues, and magnify God. Then answered Peter,* **Can any man forbid water, that these should not be baptized, which have received the Holy Ghost as well as we? And he commanded them to be baptized in the name of the Lord.** *Then prayed they him to tarry certain days.*

There is no need to try to be holy in order to receive the Holy Spirit. That is HIS work, not ours. He makes us holy after He begins flowing from our innermost being. Remember Acts 1:8 says, *"after that the Holy Ghost is come upon you . . . "*

One needs to have a hunger and thirst for more of God. If there is no interest, hunger, thirst, or desire to go deeper in God, then it will be very difficult to become fully wet, or completely covered with His Presence and Power. In other words, there will be no baptism. Being filled with, overflowing with, completely covered with the baptism of the Holy Spirit will affect every area of our lives spiritually, emotionally and even physically.

Blessed are they which do hunger and thirst after righteousness: for they shall be filled. Matthew 5:6

The next thing we must remember is to not be afraid of receiving the baptism of the Holy Spirit. God will give you that for which you ask. Fear kills any desire to go on with God; the Holy Spirit baptism is the step that begins a deeper walk with God.

If ye then, being evil, know how to give good gifts unto your children: how much more shall your heavenly Father give the Holy Spirit to them that ask him. Luke 11:13

The attitude of one's heart should be that of wanting more of Jesus, more of praising and worshipping Him that is worthy. There is no end to God and to what He has for those who desire to draw closer to Him. He is eternal.

And be not drunk with wine, wherein is excess; but be filled with the Spirit; Speaking to yourselves in psalms and hymns and spiritual songs, singing and making melody in your heart to the Lord. Ephesians 5:18-19

Evidence one has been filled

Speaking in other tongues
The first, or initial evidence one has been filled with the baptism of the Holy Spirit is speaking in other tongues, more easily understood as "a particular language." Read carefully the following references that show clearly this fact.

*And they were all filled with the Holy Ghost, and [they] began to **speak with other tongues**, as the Spirit gave them utterance.* Acts 2:4

I Would Not Have You Ignorant

And they of the circumcision which believed were astonished, as many as came with Peter, because that on the Gentiles also was poured out the gift of the Holy Ghost. For they heard them **speak with tongues**, *and magnify God.* Acts 10:45-46

He said unto them, Have ye received the Holy Ghost since ye believed? And they said unto him, We have not so much as heard whether there be any Holy Ghost. And he said unto them, Unto what then were ye baptized? And they said, Unto John's baptism. Then said Paul, John verily baptized with the baptism of repentance, saying unto the people, that they should believe on him which should come after him, that is, on Christ Jesus. When they heard this, they were baptized in the name of the Lord Jesus. And when Paul had laid his hands upon them, the Holy Ghost came on them; and they **spake with tongues**, *and prophesied.* Acts 19:2-6

These references show clearly that speaking in tongues is the initial or first evidence that one has been filled. If "joy" was the first evidence, then one would not be sure they were filled with the Holy Spirit when they wake up and find themselves in a "blue Monday" attitude. Nor would they be sure they were filled when they run out of "patience" or "love" in certain situations. But, one can know for sure that they are filled with the Holy Spirit anytime they open their mouth and speak in tongues as He gives you other words in which to praise and pray to God. A person filled with the Holy Spirit can speak in other tongues when they have no joy, love or patience and find they will soon be given the needed joy, love and patience. That is what being filled to overflowing with the Holy Spirit is all about: *" . . . rivers of living water* (the Holy Spirit) *flowing out of the belly."*

Many feel they do not have to speak in other tongues to be filled with the Holy Spirit. The choice, or will, to speak in tongues is theirs, but nevertheless, the Word of God clearly shows us that the first, initial evidence of being filled, or baptized with the Holy Spirit is speaking in other tongues. John Osteen, founder and pastor of the Lakewood Church in Houston, TX, used to say, "The baptism of the Holy Spirit is like buying a pair of new shoes: the tongues come with it." Other evidence includes:

The fruit of the Spirit
Galatians 5:22-23—*But the fruit of the Spirit is love, joy, peace, longsuffering, gentleness, goodness, faith, Meekness, temperance: against such there is no law.*

Holiness—1 Peter 1:15-16 *But as he which hath called you is holy, so be ye holy in all manner of conversation; Because it is written, Be ye holy; for I am holy.*

Boldness—Acts 4:29-31 *And now, Lord, behold their threatenings: and grant unto thy servants, that with all boldness they may speak thy word, By stretching forth thine hand to heal; and that signs and wonders may be done by the name of thy holy child Jesus. And when they had prayed, the place was shaken where they were assembled together; and they were all filled with the Holy Ghost, and they spake the word of God with boldness.*

The boldness the Holy Spirit gives us is not the kind that is blatant or repulsive, but rather a boldness described as "not being afraid" to speak up for the Lord to anyone. Acts 5:17-32 shows this principle: *"Go, stand and speak..."*

Desire to pray—Luke 4:1, 14 and 18 *And Jesus being full of the Holy Ghost returned from Jordan, and was led by the Spirit into the wilderness... And Jesus returned in the power of the Spirit into Galilee: and there went out a fame of him through all the region round about... The Spirit of the Lord is upon me, because he hath anointed me to preach the gospel to the poor; he hath sent me to heal the brokenhearted, to preach deliverance to the captives, and recovering of sight to the blind, to set at liberty them that are bruised, To preach the acceptable year of the Lord.*

Acts 4:23-33 (esp. v 31) *And being let go, they went to their own* *company, and reported all that the chief priests and elders had said unto them. And when they heard that, **they lifted up their voice to God with one accord**, and said, Lord, thou art God, which hast made heaven, and earth, and the sea, and all that in them is: Who by the mouth of thy servant David hast said, Why did the heathen rage, and the people imagine vain things? The kings of the earth stood up, and the rulers were gathered together against the Lord, and against his Christ. For of a truth against thy holy child Jesus, whom thou hast anointed, both Herod, and Pontius Pilate, with the Gentiles, and the people of Israel, were gathered together, For to do whatsoever thy hand and thy counsel determined before to be done. And now, Lord, behold their threatenings: and grant unto thy servants, that with all boldness they may speak thy word, By stretching forth thine hand to heal; and that signs and wonders may be done by the name of thy holy child Jesus. **And when they had prayed,** the place was shaken where they were assembled together; and they were all filled with the Holy Ghost, and they spake the word of God with boldness. And the multitude of them that believed were of one heart and of one soul: neither said any of them that ought of the things which he possessed was his own; but they had all things common. And with great power gave the apostles witness of the resurrection of the Lord Jesus: and great grace was upon them all.* Acts 4:24-33

Lastly, and this is perhaps the most important point to remember about the baptism of the Holy Spirit—

Acts 2:4 *" . . . **they** began to speak with other tongues, as the Spirit gave them utterance* [the words to speak].*"*

The Holy Spirit does not do the speaking in other tongues! **YOU** do!

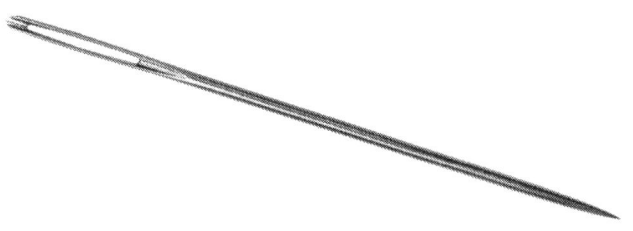

This Side or That Side of the Needle

The baptism of the Holy Spirit will take the believer through the "eye of the needle" into the vastness and glory of the unending, inexhaustible and exciting love of God.

We have our needles of Church tradition, customs, culture and denominational barriers that keep us from true fellowship with God and with one another. On THIS SIDE of the eye of the needle, we find it dark and so narrow that there is no space to move among ourselves in true fellowship. On THIS SIDE of the needle, it is very narrow because WE stand in the way; no space to let God show His glory in the church, because . . . **"we never did it that way before."** Those are the seven last words of any dying church.

But, when we "humble ourselves" and pass through the eye of the needle, we lay aside the traditions and denominational rules that have been put on us to keep us from knowing God more intimately and enter into the vastness of God's (not man's) Kingdom.

On the OTHER SIDE of the eye of the needle we find the roomy, extensive, spacious and open places of God where we find freedom, liberty, no obstacles or hindrances. We find room to move in any direction the Holy Spirit leads us. It is as though we have been *"translated out of a kingdom of darkness into the Kingdom of Light, the Kingdom of God's dear Son,"* which is made real only by the Holy Spirit.

NOW CONCERNING SPIRITUAL GIFTS

I WOULD NOT HAVE YOU IGNORANT

GIFTS of GOD

How shall we escape, if we neglect so great salvation; which at the first began to be spoken by the Lord, and was confirmed unto us by them that heard him; God also bearing them witness, both with signs and wonders, and with divers miracles, and gifts of the Holy Ghost, according to his own will? Hebrews 2:3-4

GIFTS of GOD

Salvation
Jesus answered and said unto her, If thou knewest the gift of God, and who it is that saith to thee, Give me to drink; thou wouldest have asked of him, and he would have given thee living water. John 4:10

Healing
For by grace are ye saved through faith; and that not of yourselves: it is the gift of God: Not of works, lest any man should boast. Ephesians 2:8-9

It says here that *"through faith you are saved."* The word 'saved' in *Greek* is σώζω sōzō. It means to save, that is to deliver or protect — heal, preserve, save, do well, be (or) make whole.

Holy Spirit Baptism
Acts 2:38 *Then Peter said unto them, Repent, and be baptized every one of you in the name of Jesus Christ for the remission of sins, and ye shall receive the gift of the Holy Ghost.*

From this wonderful Gift of the Holy Ghost other gifts begin to flow. There are the —

Fruit of the Spirit
Galatians 5:22-23. *But the fruit of the Spirit is love, joy, peace, longsuffering, gentleness, goodness, faith, Meekness, temperance: against such there is no law.* The number 9 is always significant of the Holy Spirit when it appears in scripture.

Gifts of the Father — measure of faith
Romans 12:1-8 *I beseech you therefore, brethren, by the mercies of God, that ye present your bodies a living sacrifice, holy, acceptable unto God, which is your reasonable service. And be not conformed to this world: but be ye transformed by the renewing of your mind, that ye may prove what is that good, and acceptable, and perfect, will of God. For I say, through the grace given unto me, to every man that is among you, not to think of himself more highly than he*

ought to think; but to think soberly, according as God hath dealt to every man the measure of faith. For as we have many members in one body, and all members have not the same office: So we, being many, are one body in Christ, and every one members one of another. Having then gifts differing according to the grace that is given to us, whether prophecy, let us prophesy according to the proportion of faith; Or ministry, let us wait on our ministering: or he that teacheth, on teaching; Or he that exhorteth, on exhortation: he that giveth, let him do it with simplicity; he that ruleth, with diligence; he that sheweth mercy, with cheerfulness.

Notice in this portion of scripture that God has *"dealt to every man the measure of faith."* This means that all men have been given a measured portion of faith. To some lots, to some little, but nonetheless there is not a person on the earth that has been without some faith. Like seeds, some are big, some are small, but ALL have the ability to produce. Now, if your measure of faith is small, all you need to do is to hear something about Jesus Christ and that measure will get bigger.

Romans 10:17 *So then faith cometh by hearing, and hearing by the word of God.*

Gifts of the Son — measure of grace
Ephesians 4:7-16 *But unto every one of us is given* **grace according to the measure of the gift of Christ**. *Wherefore he saith, When he ascended up on high, he led captivity captive, and gave gifts unto men. (Now that he ascended, what is it but that he also descended first into the lower parts of the earth? He that descended is the same also that ascended up far above all heavens, that he might fill all things.) And he gave some, apostles; and some, prophets; and some, evangelists; and some, pastors and teachers; For the perfecting of the saints, for the work of the ministry, for the edifying of the body of Christ: Till we all come in the unity of the faith, and of the knowledge of the Son of God, unto a perfect man, unto the measure of the stature of the fulness of Christ: That we henceforth be no more children, tossed to and fro, and carried about with every wind of doctrine, by the sleight of men, and cunning craftiness, whereby they lie in wait to deceive; But speaking the truth in love, may grow up*

into him in all things, which is the head, even Christ: From whom the whole body fitly joined together and compacted by that which every joint supplieth, according to the effectual working in the measure of every part, maketh increase of the body unto the edifying of itself in love.

Ephesians 2:8-9 *For by grace are ye saved through faith; and that not of yourselves: it is the gift of God. Not of works, lest any man should boast.*

Gifts of the Holy Spirit — Nine
1 Corinthians 12:1-11 *Now concerning spiritual gifts, brethren, I would not have you ignorant. Ye know that ye were Gentiles, carried away unto these dumb idols, even as ye were led. Wherefore I give you to understand, that no man speaking by the Spirit of God calleth Jesus accursed: and that no man can say that Jesus is the Lord, but by the Holy Ghost. Now there are **diversities of gifts**, but the same Spirit. And there are differences of administrations, but the same Lord. And there are diversities of operations, but it is the same God which worketh all in all. But the manifestation of the Spirit is given to every man to profit withal. For to one is given by the Spirit the **word of wisdom**; to another the **word of knowledge** by the same Spirit; To another **faith** by the same Spirit; to another the **gifts of healing** by the same Spirit; To another the **working of miracles**; to another **prophecy**; to another **discerning of spirits**; to another **divers kinds of tongues**; to another the **interpretation of tongues**: But all these worketh that one and the selfsame Spirit, dividing to every man severally as he will.*

The Holy Spirit baptism takes one deeper into the things of God. There is no end to God. We never reach a climax. There is always still more and more and more of God. BUT WITHOUT KNOWLEDGE of these wonderful gifts of the Holy Spirit, one will always remain at the same level. Hosea 4:6 mentions this principle when he said, *My people are destroyed for lack of knowledge . . .*

Until the Christian receives the baptism of the Holy Spirit, he/she may not have been ready to receive the teachings that follow in this study. But assuming that you have been filled with the Holy Spirit, now you are ready.

John 16:12-14 *I have yet many things to say unto you, but ye cannot bear them now. Howbeit when he, the Spirit of truth, is come, he will guide you into all truth: for he shall not speak of himself; but whatsoever he shall hear, that shall he speak: and he will shew you things to come. He shall glorify me: for he shall receive of mine, and shall shew it unto you.*

Mark 16:17 says, *And these signs shall follow them that believe; in my name . . . they shall speak with new tongues.*

Commenting on the above portion of Scripture, John Osteen, founding pastor/teacher of Lakewood Church in Houston, Texas, has said, "The believer's speaking in tongues is the beginning of an uncapping of ALL that the Holy Spirit has."

You Must Desire These Gifts

Paul's first letter to the Corinthian church gives details in chapters 12, 13 and 14 about the gifts of the Holy Spirit. He discusses the gifts in particular in chapter 12 and how their operation is related to physical parts of a body. He ends the chapter by saying —

But covet earnestly the best gifts: and yet shew I unto you a more excellent way . . . 1 Corinthians 12:31

Paul very clearly explains the *more excellent way* in 1 Corinthians 13:1-31. Let's read it together in order to understand just what this *more excellent way* is. It's long, but let's read it anyway. Please note and count the word "charity" **typed in bold font.** Three of the nine gifts of the Holy Spirit, prophecy, tongues and (word of) knowledge, are listed and underlined.

Though I speak with the tongues of men and of angels, and have not **charity**, *I am become as sounding brass, or a tinkling cymbal. And though I have the gift of prophecy, and understand all mysteries, and all knowledge; and though I have all faith, so that I could remove*

I Would Not Have You Ignorant

*mountains, and have not **charity**, I am nothing. And though I bestow all my goods to feed the poor, and though I give my body to be burned, and have not **charity**, it profiteth me nothing.*

***Charity** suffereth long, and is kind; **charity** envieth not; **charity** vaunteth not itself, is not puffed up, Doth not behave itself unseemly, seeketh not her own, is not easily provoked, thinketh no evil; Rejoiceth not in iniquity, but rejoiceth in the truth; Beareth all things, believeth all things, hopeth all things, endureth all things.*

***Charity** never faileth: but whether there be <u>prophecies</u>, they shall fail; whether there be <u>tongues</u>, they shall cease; whether there be <u>knowledge</u>, it shall vanish away. For we know in part, and we prophesy in part. But when that which is perfect is come, then that which is in part shall be done away.*

When I was a child, I spake as a child, I understood as a child, I thought as a child: but when I became a man, I put away childish things. For now we see through a glass, darkly; but then face to face: now I know in part; but then shall I know even as also I am known.

*And now abideth faith, hope, **charity**, these three; but the greatest of these is **charity**.*

The *"more excellent way"* is none other than charity, or in today's language, L-O-V-E. The word "charity" appears nine times here. The number nine is the number of the Holy Spirit.

— *And above all things have fervent charity among yourselves: for charity shall cover the multitude of sins.* 1 Peter 4:8

— *And above all these things put on charity, which is the bond of perfectness.* Colossians 3:14

About the gifts of prophecy, tongues, and interpretation of tongues, Paul continues his advice and teaching in chapter 14. He begins the chapter with perhaps the best advice of all — *Follow after charity, and desire spiritual gifts . . .*

There had been gross misuse of these three vocal gifts (prophecy, tongues, and interpretation of tongues) in the church bringing much confusion, which concerned Paul enough to write this letter of instruction to the Corinthian believers. Paul told the Corinthian believers, *For God is not the author of confusion, but of peace, as in all churches of the saints.* 1 Corinthians 14:33

*. . . **covet** earnestly the best gifts . . . Follow after charity, and **desire** spiritual gifts . . .* 1 Corinthians 12:31 and 1 Corinthians 14:1

Church leaders cannot covet and desire the best gifts for you. These are things you must do always remembering that LOVE must be the foundation of the operation of all the gifts of God. Notice that it says in both verses **GIFTS**, plural. There is not necessarily any limit to the number of gifts the Holy Spirit may operate through you.

*But all these worketh that one and the selfsame Spirit, dividing to every man **severally as he will**.* 1 Corinthians 12:11

Desire the gifts for the edification (uplifting, moral improvement or guidance) of the church, not for yourself. The Revised Standard Version of 1 Corinthians 12:7 emphasizes this point by saying, *"To each is given the manifestation of the Spirit for the common good."*

When you are used in the operation of the Holy Spirit's gifts, remember that you are only a vessel. The King James Version of the New Testament book titled **The Acts of the Apostles** could better be rendered as **The Acts of the Holy Spirit by the Apostles.** It will be the Holy Spirit operating His gifts through you. Again, let us emphasize that the gifts are not yours to operate as you will, but rather as the Holy Spirit wills.

NOW CONCERNING SPIRITUAL GIFTS

I WOULD NOT HAVE YOU IGNORANT

GIFTS of THE HOLY SPIRIT

"But the manifestation of the Spirit is given to every man to profit withal." 1 Corinthians 12:7

1 Corinthians 12:1-11 *Now concerning spiritual gifts, brethren, I would not have you ignorant. Ye know that ye were Gentiles, carried away unto these dumb idols, even as ye were led. Wherefore I give you to understand, that no man speaking by the Spirit of God calleth Jesus accursed: and that no man can say that Jesus is the Lord, but by the Holy Ghost. Now there are diversities of gifts, but the same Spirit. And there are differences of administrations, but the same Lord. And there are diversities of operations, but it is the same God which worketh all in all.* **But the manifestation of the Spirit is given to every man to profit withal.** *For to one is given by the Spirit the word of wisdom; to another the word of knowledge by the same Spirit; To another faith by the same Spirit; to another the gifts of healing by the same Spirit; To another the working of miracles; to another prophecy; to another discerning of spirits; to another divers kinds of tongues; to another the interpretation of tongues: But all these worketh that one and the selfsame Spirit, dividing to every man severally as he will.*

The Gifts of the Holy Spirit are nine. They are broken up into three groups of three each — utterance gifts, power gifts, and revelation gifts.

Utterance gifts include those of prophecy, tongues, and interpretation of tongues. The best of this group would be that of prophecy because it is spoken in the known language of the body of believers.

Power gifts consist of faith, working of miracles and gift(s) of healing(s), plural. The best of this three-fold group is that of faith, for without faith it is impossible for the others to manifest.

Revelation Gifts comprise the word of wisdom, the word of knowledge, and discerning of spirits, of which there are only three kinds — God's, man's and Satan's, including demons. The best of these three is the word of wisdom because it reveals the purpose and plan of God.

UTTERANCE GIFT — Prophecy

When it comes to prophecy in the Word of God, there are two kinds — the gift ministry of the prophet, and the gift of prophecy to the church body for their edification and comfort, as well as for their exhortation.

The **gift ministry of the prophet** is mentioned by Paul in his letter to the Ephesians.

Ephesians 4:11-12 *And he gave some, apostles; and some, **prophets**; and some, evangelists; and some, pastors and teachers; For the perfecting of the saints, for the work of the ministry, for the edifying of the body of Christ.*

The job, position or office of the prophet is two-fold. Firstly, he foretells the future and secondly, he guides the church by revelation from God. Ezekiel describes in detail the prophet's work or ministry.

Ezekiel 2:1-10 *And he said unto me, Son of man, stand upon thy feet, and I will speak unto thee. And the spirit entered into me when he spake unto me, and set me upon my feet, that I heard him that spake unto me. And he said unto me, Son of man, I send thee to the children of Israel, to a rebellious nation that hath rebelled against me: they and their fathers have transgressed against me, even unto this very day. For they are impudent children and stiffhearted. I do send thee unto them; and thou shalt say unto them, Thus saith the Lord God. And they, whether they will hear, or whether they will forbear, (for they are a rebellious house,) yet shall know that there hath been **a prophet** among them.*

And thou, son of man, be not afraid of them, neither be afraid of their words, though briers and thorns be with thee, and thou dost dwell among scorpions: be not afraid of their words, nor be dismayed at their looks, though they be a rebellious house. And thou shalt speak my words unto them, whether they will hear, or whether they will forbear: for they are most rebellious. But thou, son of man, hear what I say unto thee; Be not thou rebellious like that rebellious house: open thy mouth, and eat that I give thee.

And when I looked, behold, an hand was sent unto me; and, lo, a roll of a book was therein; And he spread it before me; and it was written within and without: and there was written therein lamentations, and mourning, and woe.

As mentioned earlier, **the gift of prophecy** (prophe-see) is for the whole church. The one who prophesies edifies, exhorts and comforts a church congregation. When this gift is operated it is all done in the understandable language of the congregation.

1 Corinthians 14:1-5 *Follow after charity, and desire spiritual gifts, but rather that ye may prophesy. For he that speaketh in an unknown tongue speaketh not unto men, but unto God: for no man understandeth him; howbeit in the spirit he speaketh mysteries. But he that prophesieth speaketh unto men to edification, and exhortation, and comfort. He that speaketh in an unknown tongue edifieth himself; but he that prophesieth edifieth the church. I would that ye all spake with tongues, but rather that ye prophesied: for greater is he that prophesieth than he that speaketh with tongues, except he interpret, that the church may receive edifying.*

There is a difference between the gift of the prophet to the church and the gift of prophecy.

In the Book of Acts, there is a scripture that brings out this difference very clearly. Philip, the evangelist, had four daughters **which did PROPHESY** (prophe-sigh). But after several days later, there came down from Judea **a certain PROPHET** named Agabus.

Acts 21:8-11 *And the next day we that were of Paul's company departed, and came unto Caesarea: and we entered into the house of Philip the evangelist, which was one of the seven; and abode with him. And the same man had four daughters, virgins, **which did prophesy**. And as we tarried there many days, there came down from Judaea **a certain prophet**, named Agabus. And when he was come unto us, he took Paul's girdle, and bound his own hands and feet, and said, Thus saith the Holy Ghost, So shall the Jews at Jerusalem* *bind the man that owneth this girdle, and shall deliver him into the hands of the Gentiles.*

How can prophecy (prophe-see) be defined?

Kenneth Wuest (1893-1962), a noted New Testament Greek scholar of the mid-twentieth century, in his New Testament Expanded Translation of Revelation 9:10, defines prophecy as *"the forth-telling of God's Word."* The KJV renders this scripture, *". . . for the testimony of Jesus* (concerning Jesus, about Jesus) *is the spirit of prophecy."* Jesus is the Word made flesh who dwelt among men *"telling forth"* all that His Father spoke.

All prophecy is based on the Word of God. If it does not line up with what the Bible teaches and says, then the prophecy can be questionable. God uses His Word to edify, exhort and comfort the church. Prophecy comes as God reveals or speaks His Word to the vessel (person) He is going to use to speak it forth. It begins with a word or thought, usually from the Bible.

Read the Word of God and fill yourself with it. The testimony of, about, concerning Jesus is found in the Word. This is the true spirit of prophecy. Psalm 1:2 urges one to meditate on the Word —

But his delight is in the law of the Lord; and in his law doth he meditate day and night.

How can one expect the gift to operate?
The Holy Spirit will begin by speaking a word or thought, usually from the Bible, to your heart (mind). He will often repeat the word or thought, sometimes adding to it little by little.

Many times the entire message is NOT given to the person whom God is about to use. You will find that as you step out in FAITH to speak, the Holy Spirit will give the rest automatically.

As you begin to speak, the anointing comes upon you to speak with authority from God. People will know it is God and not you.

I Would Not Have You Ignorant

UTTERANCE GIFT — Tongues

W. W. Patterson, former missionary to Indonesia and pastor of Bethel Temple in Seattle, Washington, published **"Speaking In Tongues, Sign and Gift"** in 1943. The booklet brought such understanding concerning the difference between 1) the tongues manifest in the Baptism of the Holy Spirit and 2) the Gift of Tongues spoken of by Paul in his first Corinthian letter, that it was re-published again in 1957 and 1965. The booklet is now out of print but is available online in PDF format for easy downloading at http://www.bfi-online.org/wp-content/uploads/2012/04/Speaking-in-Tongues-WWPatterson.pdf.

There are two kinds of tongues as mentioned above:

First, there is **the SIGN** of the believer being filled with the Holy Spirit is initially evidenced by speaking in tongues.

Acts 1:12-15 *Then returned **they** unto Jerusalem from the mount called Olivet, which is from Jerusalem a sabbath day's journey. And when **they** were come in, **they** went up into an upper room, where abode both Peter, and James, and John, and Andrew, Philip, and Thomas, Bartholomew, and Matthew, James the son of Alphaeus, and Simon Zelotes, and Judas the brother of James. **These** all continued with one accord in prayer and supplication, with the women, and Mary the mother of Jesus, and with his brethren. And in those days Peter stood up in the midst of the disciples, and said,* **(the number of names together were about an hundred and twenty)**.

The reason we quote the scripture above is that there were about 120 believers gathered together in the upper room on the day of Pentecost. Now let's continue reading in Acts 2:1-4 where it describes very clearly what happened on the day of Pentecost.

*And when the day of Pentecost was fully come, **they** were all with one accord in one place. And suddenly there came a sound from heaven as of a rushing mighty wind, and it filled all the house where **they** were sitting. And there appeared unto **them** cloven tongues like* *as of fire, and it sat upon each of **them**. And **they** were all filled with the Holy Ghost, and began to speak with other tongues, as the Spirit gave them utterance.*

All 120 believers were filled with the Holy Spirit on the Day of Pentecost and *"began to speak with other tongues, as the Spirit gave them utterance."* This shows clearly that the initial evidence of being filled with the Holy Ghost is speaking in tongues. There was no limit that day in the number of believers who could speak in tongues. PLUS before the day was over another some 3,000 were added to the church; then a few days after that, another 5,000. These more than 8,000 had simply responded to Peter's advice of what to do to be saved.

Acts 2:38-41 *Then Peter said unto them,* **Repent**, *and* **be baptized** (in water) *every one of you in the name of Jesus Christ for the remission of sins,* **and ye shall receive the gift of the Holy Ghost.** *For the promise is unto you, and to your children, and to all that are afar off, even as many as the Lord our God shall call. And with many other words did he testify and exhort, saying, Save yourselves from this untoward generation. Then they that gladly received his word were baptized: and the same day there were added unto them about* **three thousand souls**.

Acts 4:4 *Howbeit many of them which heard the word believed; and the number of the men was* **about five thousand**.

The Baptism of the Holy Spirit is for any believer, all believers. There is no limit on the number of people who can speak in tongues.

What this experience (speaking in tongues as the initial sign of being filled with the Holy Spirit) does for the believer is that it will **personally edify**. Edify is an old English word that implies "constructive instruction that builds up or improves," in this case, an individual.

1 Corinthians 14:4 *He that speaketh in an unknown tongue edifieth himself; but he that prophesieth edifieth the church.*

I Would Not Have You Ignorant

No one can understand this tongue except the Holy Spirit, who may **personally reveal** (interpret) the meaning to the believer while the individual is intimately waiting on God in prayer or communion.

By praying in this tongue regularly, one's spirit is **personally encouraged and comforted.** There is power in your prayer-communion language.

So, in essence, there is no limit to the number of people who can speak in tongues when it comes to the Baptism of the Holy Spirit. In a church service ALL can sing, ALL can pray, and ALL can worship in tongues to God.

The Power of Language

Genesis 11:1 says, *"And the whole earth was of one language, and one speech."*

Can you imagine? From God's creation of Adam & Eve to the Tower of Babel, every human being on the globe at that time spoke the same, original language that God gave to Adam & Eve. We can liken that one language to a complete, **clear, see-through glass**. Everyone who spoke it had no communication problem because they spoke the same language. There were absolutely no misunderstandings. It was a perfect language. After all, it was God in the first place Who gave His way of speaking and communicating to the first couple. It was perfect.

God had directed the people to disperse, but they refused and began building themselves a tower, a name for themselves.

Genesis 11:6 (Good News Bible) *God said, Now then, these are all one people and they speak one language; this is just the beginning of what they are going to do. Soon they will be able to do anything they want! Let us go down and mix up their language so that they will not understand each other.*

The reason they would be able to do anything they wanted was that their language was one. They were in complete unity because of their language. I look at and explain it this way: God took the GLASS of HIS PERFECT LANGUAGE and smashed it to the ground, breaking it into 6,900 pieces (of languages on the earth), some big, some small, some even minute.

It was then the people camped in the plains of Shinar picked up their piece of the original language and migrated to a place where they all spoke the same piece. Their piece of God's original language became "the expression or communication of their thoughts and feelings." I can imagine, like Ernest Gentile once said, "God scrambled their brains as well as their language." The thoughts and communication between all these people became impossible, thus demanding their dispersion.

And so, the people were dispersed and the world became populated. Had their language remained that *"one language and one speech,"* that God had originally given to man in the beginning up until the event in the plain of Shinar nothing would have been impossible for those people to do.

Jesus' last words were, *"But ye shall receive power, after that the Holy Ghost is come upon you."*

They went to Jerusalem, waited ten days, and on that momentous day, when they were ALL with ONE ACCORD, unified, *"Suddenly there came a sound from heaven as of a rushing mighty wind, and it filled all the house where they were sitting . . . And they were all filled with the Holy Ghost, and began to speak with other tongues, as the Spirit gave them utterance."*

They all began to speak the *"wonderful works of God."* It was in that moment . . .

I believe that God brought together all the pieces of known languages on the earth into one piece and restored the broken *"one language and one speech"* that He had originally bestowed to Adam and Eve at their creation, and gave it to the newly-birthed church on the Day of Pentecost.

The spirits of those who are filled

with the Holy Spirit and speak in tongues are in perfect unity with God. 1 Corinthians 14:2 says, *For he that speaketh in an unknown tongue speaketh not unto men, but unto God: for no man understandeth him; howbeit in the spirit* (i.e. his own spirit) *he speaketh mysteries* (to God).

Because of this *"one language and one speech"* of the Holy Spirit, I believe all things are made possible to those who believe! **Nothing shall be withheld from those who believe**. With God, all things are possible. *"The things which are impossible with men are possible with God."* Luke 18:27

Have YOU received the Holy Ghost since YOU believed?

Secondly, **the GIFT** of tongues is given by the Holy Spirit for the express purpose of edifying and comforting the corporate body of believers called the church. This gift is different than the Holy Spirit Baptism which is evidenced by speaking in tongues.

1 Corinthians 14:5 *I would that ye all spake with tongues, but rather that ye prophesied: for greater is he that prophesieth than he that speaketh with tongues, except he interpret,* **that the church may receive edifying.**

1 Corinthians 14:12-15 *Even so ye, forasmuch as ye are zealous of spiritual gifts, seek that ye may excel to* **the edifying of the church**. *Wherefore let him that speaketh in an unknown tongue pray that he may interpret. For if I pray in an unknown tongue, my spirit prayeth, but my understanding is unfruitful. What is it then? I will pray with the spirit, and I will pray with the understanding also: I will sing with the spirit, and I will sing with the understanding also.*

The Gift of Tongues is NOT given to all, as in the Baptism of the Holy Spirit mentioned above, but rather only to those whom the Holy Spirit wills.

1 Corinthians 12:10 *To another the working of miracles; to another prophecy; to another discerning of spirits;* **to another divers kinds of tongues**; *to another the interpretation of tongues.*

I Would Not Have You Ignorant

UTTERANCE GIFT — Interpretation of Tongues

The word **"interpret"** means to untie, unfasten, unravel something that is said in a foreign language. In the operation of this gift time is spent untying, undoing, unraveling, loosening the message spoken in tongues. It is an interpretation NOT a translation. The message may not be interpreted word-for-word, but rather the Holy Spirit unravels, unties, loosens, unfastens the message into the known language of the congregation so that they all may benefit by it.

When a message in tongues is given and it seems to be very long, followed by a much shorter interpretation, there is no need to be alarmed. One must remember what is spoken in a foreign language may very well be interpreted by the Holy Spirit in much shorter phrases. Foreign languages are like that. For example, it takes seven words in English to say, "Tomorrow I will go to the store," but spoken in Japanese only four words are necessary to say exactly the same thing. "Ashita mise ni ikimasu." In the language of an unreached tribe living in the jungles of Papua New Guinea, it may take even fewer words.

Once again, a message in tongues is interpreted (unfastend, unraveled, untied) into the common language of the congregation. It is NOT translated.

A message in tongues accompanied by the interpretation thereof would be the same as the gift of prophecy spoken in the common language of the congregation. Oftentimes if one is used in one of these utterance gifts, the Holy Spirit can, and sometimes will use the person in all three.

Operation of the gift of tongues and interpretation

Message in Tongues
Each case is different but what one could very well experience is the Presence of God, otherwise termed as *the anointing*. It begins moving on the inside (the abdomen, belly, gut). As this increases, one may possibly begin shaking on the inside as the breathing increases. The breathing may increase to a point where your lips may even begin to quiver. This experience is the Holy Spirit Himself preparing you with confidence that it is He who wants to speak to the congregation. There is no thought or word that accompanies this anointing.

As you step out in FAITH to speak, the Holy Spirit will give you the (foreign) words to speak. He knows when to stop speaking.

If you are experiencing these feelings of preparation during praise and worship, it is best to wait until there is an opening where the worship leader pauses to wait on the Holy Spirit. Usually, during the time of worship, the hearts of the congregation are also being prepared to receive an edifying word from God. When it becomes quiet before the Lord, then step out and let the Holy Spirit speak through you in a message in tongues. The Holy Spirit will also be preparing another person in the congregation with the interpretation.

Many times, just as the song service does, the message in tongues accompanied by an interpretation will confirm the pastor's message that follows. This will encourage the congregation to know that both the worship leader and the Holy Spirit are in unity concerning the message that is about to be preached to the entire congregation.

Another time the Gift of Tongues and Interpretation will manifest is at the end of a pastoral message. He will confirm the Word that was spoken with these supernatural gifts. There will usually be a time of prayer or quiet as the message comes to an end. This will allow the Holy Spirit to prepare the person He will use to edify the congregation.

I Would Not Have You Ignorant

Waiting on the Holy Spirit is very important. We must learn to give Him time, to allow Him time to minister in our church congregations. Many times we get so involved in the time element of a service that we rush to get done so we can go on with OUR planned activities.

Interpretation of Tongues
The operation of the gift of interpretation is the same as that of the gift of prophecy. Namely, the Holy Spirit will begin by speaking a word or thought, usually from the Bible, to your heart (mind). He will often repeat the word or thought, sometimes adding to it little by little.

The entire interpretation may NOT be given to the person whom God is about to use. One will find that as they step out in FAITH to speak, the Holy Spirit will give the rest automatically. As the individual begins to speak, the anointing comes upon them to speak with authority from God. People will know it is God.

Limits
The Word of God establishes certain limits to the number of prophecies and messages in tongues coupled with the interpretations. There was much, much confusion in the Corinthian church concerning the operation of these gifts, so Paul wrote specific instructions to the church to bring order. He begins in 1 Corinthians 14:27 and 2 Corinthians 13:1 by referring to the Old Testament scriptures found in Deuteronomy 17:6 and 19:15. Jesus also makes mention of these scriptures in Matthew 18:16 and John 8:17. We list them here for your easy reference. These scriptures all show the principle of God's Word being established in the mouths of two, or at the most by three.

Paul: 1 Corinthians 14:27 *If any man speak in an unknown tongue, let it be by two, or at the most by three, and that by course; and let one interpret.*

Paul: 2 Corinthians 13:1 *This is the third time I am coming to you. In the mouth of two or three witnesses shall every word be established.*

Moses: Deuteronomy 17:6 *At the mouth of two witnesses, or three witnesses, shall he that is worthy of death be put to death; but at the mouth of one witness he shall not be put to death.*

Moses: Deuteronomy 19:15 *One witness shall not rise up against a man for any iniquity, or for any sin, in any sin that he sinneth: at the mouth of two witnesses, or at the mouth of three witnesses, shall the matter be established.*

Jesus: Matthew 18:16 *But if he will not hear thee, then take with thee one or two more, that in the mouth of two or three witnesses every word may be established.*

Jesus: John 8:17 *It is also written in your law, that the testimony of two men is true.*

However, when there are more than three vocal manifestations, be careful not to limit God, because a "WORD of wisdom," or a "WORD of knowledge" can also be spoken by and or through the gifts of prophecy, tongues, and interpretation. Therefore, it is very important to LISTEN TO THE CONTENT of each vocal manifestation to determine which gift is operating.

A prophecy or message(s) in tongues coupled with the interpretation will build up and encourage the people who are presently gathered in the corporate worship service. A word of knowledge will either refer to something past, or present, while on the other hand a word of wisdom will refer to the purpose and plan of God in the future tense.

Be encouraged
God desires to use you in the gifts of the Holy Spirit. DO NOT BE AFRAID. God will prepare your heart with a word or sign first. This gives you room to step out in faith and speak. Remember that fear kills faith.

Please read these scriptures from the Amplified Bible for a better understanding of how we should respond in order to allow the Holy Spirit to operate His gifts through us:

I Would Not Have You Ignorant

2 Timothy 1:6-7 *That is why I would remind you to stir up — rekindle the embers, fan the flame and keep burning — the* [gracious] *gift of God,* [the inner fire] *that is in you by means of the laying on of my hands* [with those of the elders at your ordination]. *For God did not give us a spirit of timidity — of cowardice, of craven and cringing and fawning fear — but* [He has given us a spirit] *of power and of love and of calm and well-balanced mind and discipline and self-control.*

Romans 12:6 *Having gifts* (faculties, talents, qualities) *that differ according to the grace given us, let us use them:* [He whose gift is] *prophecy,* [let him prophesy] **according to the proportion of his faith.**

The Japanese translation renders this portion of Romans 12:6 as *"respond to faith and prophesy."*

If leadership spent more time waiting for God during praise and worship, or at the end of the service in a time of response, it would be much easier to move in the operations of the gifts of the Holy Spirit. Let's try it and see what God will do! We must create time in our services for God to make Himself known among us. It is HIS worship, not ours.

POWER GIFT — Faith

There are three kinds of faith: saving faith, general faith and the (Holy Spirit's) gift of faith described by Paul in 1 Corinthians 12:9 in the list of the nine gifts of the Holy Spirit.

Saving faith
This kind of faith is for anyone. It is given to us by the Word of God.

Romans 10:17 *So then faith cometh by hearing, and hearing by the word of God.*

Ephesians 2:8 *For by grace are ye saved through faith; and that not of yourselves: **it** is the gift of God.*

The word "it" refers here to "faith" being a gift of God. Saving faith comes to us by (as a result of) hearing the Word of God being spoken. It grows and develops as we come to understand Christ. Romans 10:14-18 and 1 Peter 1:23-25 show clearly that saving faith comes before the salvation experience. It comes by hearing the Word of God, by hearing a Word about Jesus Christ.

Romans 10:14-18 *How then shall they call on him in whom they have not believed? and how shall they believe in him of whom they have not heard? and how shall they hear without a preacher? And how shall they preach, except they be sent? as it is written, How beautiful are the feet of them that preach the gospel of peace, and bring glad tidings of good things! But they have not all obeyed the gospel. For Esaias saith, Lord, who hath believed our report? So then faith cometh by hearing, and hearing by the word of God. But I say, Have they not heard? Yes verily, their sound went into all the earth, and their words unto the ends of the world.*

1 Peter 1:23-25 *Being born again, not of corruptible seed, but of incorruptible, by the word of God, which liveth and abideth for ever. For all flesh is as grass, and all the glory of man as the flower of grass. The grass withereth, and the flower thereof falleth away: But the word of the Lord endureth for ever. And this is the word which*

I Would Not Have You Ignorant

by the gospel is preached unto you.

General faith
Romans 12:3b says, *". . . but to think soberly according as God has dealt to every man the measure of faith."* All believers have been given this general faith. General faith is made known in our daily Christian life in PRAYER. Notice that it says, *"God has dealt to **every man** the **measure** of faith."* It is called "the measure of faith" indicating there are degrees.

Mark 11:22-24 *And Jesus answering saith unto them, Have faith in God. For verily I say unto you, That whosoever shall say unto this mountain, Be thou removed, and be thou cast into the sea; and shall not doubt in his heart, but shall believe that those things which he saith shall come to pass; he shall have whatsoever he saith. Therefore I say unto you, What things soever ye desire, **when ye pray**, believe that ye receive them, and ye shall have them.*

Through this faith, one receives answers to prayer. General faith increases and bears more fruit as we feed on the Word of God. We can develop our faith by reading the Word, quoting it in our prayers, and even singing it like David did in the Book of Psalms. Paul encouraged the Ephesian believers to be filled with the Holy Spirit *"speaking to yourselves in psalms . . ."* The early believers used the Book of Psalms as their hymnbook. It was not only a songbook but a book of poetry as well, that built the faith of early church believers.

The Holy Spirit's gift of faith
A word from God requiring action on the hearer's part is needed in order for the Holy Spirit to operate this gift. In the life of Jesus, we note that He always heard from God and responded.

John 5:19-20 *Then answered Jesus and said unto them, Verily, verily, I say unto you, The Son can do nothing of himself, but what he seeth the Father do: for what things soever he doeth, these also doeth the Son likewise. For the Father loveth the Son, and sheweth him all things that himself doeth: and he will shew him greater works than these, that ye may marvel.*

John 8:28-29 *Then said Jesus unto them, When ye have lifted up the Son of man, then shall ye know that I am he, and that I do nothing of myself; but as my Father hath taught me, I speak these things. And he that sent me is with me: the Father hath not left me alone; for I do always those things that please him.*

Paul perceived by a word from God — Acts 14:8-10 *And there sat a certain man at Lystra, impotent in his feet, being a cripple from his mother's womb, who never had walked: The same heard Paul speak: who stedfastly beholding him, and perceiving that he had faith to be healed, Said with a loud voice, Stand upright on thy feet. And he leaped and walked.*

Paul filled with the Holy Spirit was told by a word what would happen, stepped out in faith and spoke — Acts 13:8-12 *But Elymas the sorcerer (for so is his name by interpretation) withstood them, seeking to turn away the deputy from the faith. Then Saul, (who also is called Paul,) filled with the Holy Ghost, set his eyes on him, And said, O full of all subtilty and all mischief, thou child of the devil, thou enemy of all righteousness, wilt thou not cease to pervert the right ways of the Lord? And now, behold, the hand of the Lord is upon thee, and thou shalt be blind, not seeing the sun for a season. And immediately there fell on him a mist and a darkness; and he went about seeking some to lead him by the hand. Then the deputy, when he saw what was done, believed, being astonished at the doctrine of the Lord.*

Paul gave a word of faith to the people in the boat — Acts 27:21-25 *But after long abstinence Paul stood forth in the midst of them, and said, Sirs, ye should have hearkened unto me, and not have loosed from Crete, and to have gained this harm and loss. And now I exhort you to be of good cheer: for there shall be no loss of any man's life among you, but of the ship. For there stood by me this night the angel of God, whose I am, and whom I serve, Saying, Fear not, Paul; thou must be brought before Caesar: and, lo, God hath given thee all them that sail with thee. Wherefore, sirs, be of good cheer: for I believe God, that it shall be even as it was told me.*

We notice that in all these examples 1) a word [of faith] was spoken by the Holy Spirit to one's heart; 2) that person had to then obey by either speaking or doing what the Holy Spirit directed. As a result 3) something miraculous occurred. This gift of faith cannot operate unless there is an obedient response.

The gift of faith may be manifested by way of the written Word of God, dreams, visions, or the inner voice of the Holy Spirit.

The FAITH Chapter of the Bible, Hebrews 11, shows this principle here, that is, a word being spoken by God requiring obedience to what is asked by the Holy Spirit in order for a miracle or healing to take place.

Hebrews 11:7 Noah acted in faith at a word from God — *By faith Noah, being warned of God of things not seen as yet, moved with fear, prepared an ark to the saving of his house; by the which he condemned the world, and became heir of the righteousness which is by faith.*

Hebrews 11:8 Abraham's going out Ur was because of a word from God, requiring him to leave — *By faith Abraham, when he was called to go out into a place which he should after receive for an inheritance, obeyed; and he went out, not knowing whither he went.*

Hebrews 11:11 Sarah believed she could have a child because of a word from God. Note that the word required Abraham and Sarah to have sex even though they were way past the age. God did the impossible after they acted (had sex) in faith believing they would conceive — *Through faith also Sara herself received strength to conceive seed, and was delivered of a child when she was past age, because she judged him faithful who had promised.*

Hebrews 11:30 Israel destroyed the walls of Jericho because God had revealed to them His plan by a word — *By faith the walls of Jericho fell down, after they were compassed about seven days.*

Operation of the gift of faith

As a result of what we have learned so far, we see a pattern and can understand just how the Holy Spirit's gift of faith operates.

God, The Holy Spirit, 1) **speaks a word** of faith to an individual **requiring some kind of action**. Once the person receiving that word is 2) **obedient** and follows through **by doing what the word requires**, then 3) **miracles, wonders, and healing(s) occur**.

The gift of faith works together with the working of miracles, gift(s) of healing(s), a word of knowledge, and sometimes even a word of wisdom and discerning of spirits. The gift of faith is needed to see all these gifts operate in the church.

Charles Peter Wagner, Christian theologian, missiologist, missionary, writer, teacher, and church growth specialist, best known for his controversial writings on spiritual warfare suggests that "a person with this gift also is very interested in the future rather than the past. They are goal-centered. They see church growth and development as possible even when circumstances show the opposite. To a person with this gift, the impossible is possible because of what the Word of God says."

Wagner quotes Kenneth Kinghorn, warning, "The person who has the [Holy Spirit's] gift of faith should not chide others for their lack of faith. After all, not every Christian possesses this gift."

POWER GIFT — Working of Miracles

Kenneth Hagin, an influential American Pentecostal preacher and often referred to as the "father" of the "Word of Faith" movement said, "Water turned into wine by the process of nature is a natural miracle, but water turned into wine by speaking a word, as Jesus did in John 2:1-11, is the meaning of the spiritual gift of the working of

I Would Not Have You Ignorant

miracles."

In defining the word "miracles" in Greek, Hagin points out that miracles are "explosions of almightiness; impelling, staggering wonders and astonishment." Simply stated then, the working of miracles can be defined as "the power, ability, and/or strength to do explosions of almightiness."

A pioneer in the Pentecostal Christian faith, Howard Carter in his book *Questions and Answers on Spiritual Gifts*, says, "The working of miracles is a very important manifestation of the Spirit. It is the mighty power of God flowing through a person."

The Greek word for "miracle" is one most all Christians know — δύναμις dynamis dü'-nä-mēs. It is from this word we get the English word "dynamite." It means strength, power, force, and ability. Therefore, when God does a miracle, His power to alter nature is manifest. A miracle is a working of power by God!

Kinds of miracles

There are two kinds of miracles found in the Word of God: those that change the course or process of nature, and healing miracles. Let us look at some Old Testament miracles that changed the ordinary course or process of nature.

Be sure to look at the bold type and note that a Word is spoken by God requiring action to be taken before the miracle occurs. Let's recall that just before Jesus turned water into wine at the wedding feast in Cana, his mother Mary shared with the servants perhaps the most important prerequisite to having a miracle of God occur. She said emphatically, *"Whatsoever he saith unto you, do it."*

Plagues in Egypt

Exodus 7:19-20 BLOOD
And the Lord spake unto Moses, **Say** *unto Aaron,* **Take thy rod, and stretch out thine hand upon the waters of Egypt,** *upon their streams, upon their rivers, and upon their ponds, and upon all their pools of water, that they may become blood; and that there may be*

blood throughout all the land of Egypt, both in vessels of wood, and in vessels of stone. And Moses and Aaron did so, as the Lord commanded; and he lifted up the rod, and smote the waters that were in the river, in the sight of Pharaoh, and in the sight of his servants; **and all the waters that were in the river were turned to blood.**

Exodus 8:5-7 FROGS
And the Lord spake unto Moses, **Say** *unto Aaron,* **Stretch forth thine hand with thy rod over the streams, over the rivers, and over the ponds,** *and cause frogs to come up upon the land of Egypt. And Aaron stretched out his hand over the waters of Egypt;* **and the frogs came up, and covered the land of Egypt.** *And the magicians did so with their enchantments, and brought up frogs upon the land of Egypt.*

Exodus 8:16-17 LICE
And the Lord said unto Moses, **Say** *unto Aaron,* **Stretch out thy rod, and smite the dust of the land***, that it may become lice throughout all the land of Egypt. And they did so; for Aaron stretched out his hand with his rod, and smote the dust of the earth, and* **it became lice in man, and in beast; all the dust of the land became lice throughout all the land of Egypt***.*

Exodus 9:8-12 BOILS *And the Lord said unto Moses and unto Aaron,* **Take to you handfuls of ashes of the furnace, and let Moses sprinkle it toward the heaven in the sight of Pharaoh.** *And it shall become small dust in all the land of Egypt, and shall be a boil breaking forth with blains upon man, and upon beast, throughout all the land of Egypt. And* **they took ashes of the furnace, and stood before Pharaoh; and Moses sprinkled it up toward heaven; and it became a boil breaking forth with blains upon man, and upon beast.** *And the magicians could not stand before Moses because of the boils; for the boil was upon the magicians, and upon all the Egyptians. And the Lord hardened the heart of Pharaoh, and he hearkened not unto them; as the Lord had spoken unto Moses.*

Exodus 9:22-26 HAIL
And the Lord said unto Moses, **Stretch forth thine hand toward**

I Would Not Have You Ignorant

heaven, that there may be hail in all the land of Egypt, upon man, and upon beast, and upon every herb of the field, throughout the land of Egypt. And **Moses stretched forth his rod toward heaven:** *and the Lord sent thunder and hail, and the fire ran along upon the ground; and the Lord rained hail upon the land of Egypt.* **So there was hail, and fire mingled with the hail, very grievous, such as there was none like it in all the land of Egypt since it became a nation.** *And the hail smote throughout all the land of Egypt all that was in the field, both man and beast; and the hail smote every herb of the field, and brake every tree of the field. Only in the land of Goshen, where the children of Israel were, was there no hail.*

Exodus 10:12-15 LOCUSTS
And the Lord said unto Moses, **Stretch out thine hand over the land of Egypt for the locusts, that they may come up upon the land of Egypt, and eat every herb of the land, even all that the hail hath left.** *And* **Moses stretched forth his rod** *over the land of Egypt, and the Lord brought an east wind upon the land all that day, and all that night; and when it was morning,* **the east wind brought the locusts. And the locusts went up over all the land of Egypt,** *and rested in all the coasts of Egypt: very grievous were they; before them there were no such locusts as they, neither after them shall be such. For they covered the face of the whole earth, so that the land was darkened; and they did eat every herb of the land, and all the fruit of the trees which the hail had left: and there remained not any green thing in the trees, or in the herbs of the field, through all the land of Egypt.*

Exodus 10:21-23 DARKNESS
And the Lord said unto Moses, **Stretch out thine hand toward heaven, that there may be darkness over the land of Egypt,** *even darkness which may be felt. And* **Moses stretched forth his hand** *toward heaven;* **and there was a thick darkness in all the land of Egypt three days**: *They saw not one another, neither rose any from his place for three days: but all the children of Israel had light in their dwellings.*

Exodus 11:1-6 DEATH
And the Lord said unto Moses, Yet will I bring one plague more

upon Pharaoh, and upon Egypt; afterwards he will let you go hence: when he shall let you go, he shall surely thrust you out hence altogether. **Speak now in the ears of the people,** *and let every man borrow of his neighbour, and every woman of her neighbour, jewels of silver, and jewels of gold. And the Lord gave the people favour in the sight of the Egyptians. Moreover the man* **Moses was very great in the land of Egypt, in the sight of Pharaoh's servants, and in the sight of the people. And Moses said,** *Thus saith the Lord, About midnight will I go out into the midst of Egypt: And all the firstborn in the land of Egypt shall die, from the firstborn of Pharaoh that sitteth upon his throne, even unto the firstborn of the maidservant that is behind the mill; and all the firstborn of beasts. And there shall be a great cry throughout all the land of Egypt, such as there was none like it, nor shall be like it any more.*

Notice that in Exodus 12 important directions for the safety of families in Israel were given. Those directions had to be **obeyed** in order for God to reveal His miraculous power of deliverance out of Egypt and across the Red Sea.

Moses always obeyed a word or spoke a word from God. He obeyed the "Word of Faith" and miracles that altered the course of nature occurred.

Red Sea Deliverance
Exodus 14:16, 21-31 **But lift thou up thy rod, and stretch out thine hand over the sea, and divide it**: *and the children of Israel shall go on dry ground through the midst of the sea. And* **Moses stretched out his hand over the sea**; *and the Lord caused the sea to go back by a strong east wind all that night, and made the sea dry land,* **and the waters were divided**. *And the children of Israel went into the midst of the sea upon the dry ground: and the waters were a wall unto them on their right hand, and on their left.*

And the Egyptians pursued, and went in after them to the midst of the sea, even all Pharaoh's horses, his chariots, and his horsemen. And it came to pass, that in the morning watch the Lord looked unto the host of the Egyptians through the pillar of fire and of the cloud, and troubled the host of the Egyptians, And took off their chariot wheels, that they drave them heavily: so that the Egyptians said, Let us flee from the face of Israel; for the Lord fighteth for them against the Egyptians.

And the Lord said unto Moses, **Stretch out thine hand over the sea, that the waters may come again upon the Egyptians**, *upon their chariots, and upon their horsemen.* **And Moses stretched forth his hand over the sea, and the sea returned to his strength when the morning appeared**; *and the Egyptians fled against it; and the Lord overthrew the Egyptians in the midst of the sea. And the waters returned, and covered the chariots, and the horsemen, and all the host of Pharaoh that came into the sea after them; there remained not so much as one of them. But the children of Israel walked upon dry land in the midst of the sea; and the waters were a wall unto them on their right hand, and on their left. Thus the Lord saved Israel that day out of the hand of the Egyptians; and Israel saw the Egyptians dead upon the sea shore. And Israel saw that great work which the Lord did upon the Egyptians: and the people feared the Lord, and believed the Lord, and his servant Moses.*

Meal and Oil

1 Kings 17:12-16 *So he* (Elijah) *arose and went to Zarephath. And when he came to the gate of the city, behold, the widow woman was there gathering of sticks: and he called to her, and said,* **Fetch me, I pray thee, a little water in a vessel, that I may drink. And as she was going to fetch it, he called to her, and said, Bring me, I pray thee, a morsel of bread in thine hand**. *And she said, As the Lord thy God liveth, I have not a cake, but an handful of meal in a barrel, and a little oil in a cruse: and, behold, I am gathering two sticks, that I may go in and dress it for me and my son, that we may eat it, and die. And Elijah said unto her, Fear not; go and do as thou hast said:* **but make me thereof a little cake first, and bring it unto me, and after make for thee and for thy son. For thus saith the Lord God of Israel, The barrel of meal shall not waste, neither shall the cruse of oil fail, until the day that the Lord sendeth rain upon the earth.** *And* **she went and did according to the saying of Elijah**: *and she, and he, and her house, did eat many days.* **And the barrel of meal wasted not, neither did the cruse of oil fail, according to the word of the Lord**, *which he spake by Elijah.*

Elijah (Jehovah is God) the prophet of God spoke a word, the woman obeyed, and a miracle that changed the course of nature happened.

Now, let's turn to the New Testament and look at some of the miracles that are recorded there.

John 2:1-11 WATER INTO WINE
*And the third day there was a marriage in Cana of Galilee; and the mother of Jesus was there: And both Jesus was called, and his disciples, to the marriage. And when they wanted wine, the mother of Jesus saith unto him, They have no wine. Jesus saith unto her, Woman, what have I to do with thee? mine hour is not yet come. His mother saith unto the servants, **Whatsoever he saith unto you, do it**. And there were set there six waterpots of stone, after the manner of the purifying of the Jews, containing two or three firkins apiece. **Jesus saith unto them, Fill the waterpots with water**. And they filled them up to the brim. And **he saith unto them, Draw out now, and bear unto the governor of the feast**. **And they bare it**. When the ruler of the feast had **tasted the water that was made wine**, and knew not whence it was: (but the servants which drew the water knew;) the governor of the feast called the bridegroom, And saith unto him, Every man at the beginning doth set forth good wine; and when men have well drunk, then that which is worse: but thou hast kept the good wine until now. This beginning of miracles did Jesus in Cana of Galilee, and manifested forth his glory; and his disciples believed on him.*

By obeying the directive words of Jesus to fill waterpots, and draw out and take the wine to the governor of the feast, the miracle occurred. This turning of water into wine was the beginning of miracles in the three and a half year ministry of Jesus. People BELIEVED as a result. Miracles will cause doubting people to believe in Jesus Christ as Lord.

Mark 4:39 WIND AND SEA
*And he arose, and rebuked the wind, and **said unto the sea, Peace, be still**. And **the wind ceased**, and there was a great calm.*

Jesus spoke a word to the wind and sea. They obeyed, and a miracle that literally changed the course of nature happened.

Acts 6:5-8 STEPHEN

And the saying pleased the whole multitude: and they chose **Stephen, a man full of faith and of the Holy Ghost,** *and Philip, and Prochorus, and Nicanor, and Timon, and Parmenas, and Nicolas a proselyte of Antioch: Whom they set before the apostles: and when they had prayed, they laid their hands on them. And the word of God increased; and the number of the disciples multiplied in Jerusalem greatly; and a great company of the priests were obedient to the faith.* **And Stephen, full of faith and power,** *did great wonders and miracles among the people.*

Stephen, full of faith and **power (i.e. dunamis)** did great wonders and miracles among the people. Notice also verse 5 where it states Stephen was a man full of FAITH and the HOLY SPIRIT. The Holy Spirit operated His gift of faith through Stephen.

Acts 8:5-8 PHILIP

Then Philip went down to the city of Samaria, and preached Christ unto them. And the people with one accord gave heed unto those things which Philip spake, hearing and seeing the miracles which he did. For unclean spirits, crying with loud voice, came out of many that were possessed with them: and many taken with palsies, and that were lame, were healed. And there was great joy in that city.

The Holy Spirit did miracles and healed the sick through Philip. All three power gifts (faith, working of miracles and gift(s) of healing(s)) operated here.

Acts 19:11 We notice also that *God wrought special miracles by the hands of PAUL.*

Acts 15:12 BARNABAS & PAUL

Then all the multitude kept silence, and gave audience to Barnabas and Paul, declaring what miracles and wonders God had wrought among the Gentiles by them.

There is a common factor that appears in each of the Old Testament and New Testament examples listed here. This common factor explains how the gift of the working of miracles operates. The Holy Spirit SPEAKS A WORD requiring some kind of action. A human vessel RECEIVES and OBEYS by responding to that word. The miracle OCCURS.

There is a similarity in the operation of the working of miracles and the gift of faith. It is the author's belief that the word spoken in the operation of the gift of the working of miracles requiring a response from the receiver is that of a word of faith. Faith is necessary to see the impossible come to pass. Faith without a response produces nothing. Cf. James 2:20, 26 where is says, *But wilt thou know, O vain man, that faith without works is dead? . . . For as the body without the spirit is dead, so faith without works is dead also.*

Hebrews 11:11 (Amplified) *Because of faith also Sarah herself received physical power to conceive a child, even when she was long past the age for it, because she considered (God) Who had given her the promise, reliable and trustworthy and true to His Word.*

Sarah had herself a baby at almost 100 years of age! This kind of miracle would certainly be way beyond the course of nature. God spoke to Abraham and his wife saying they would have a baby in about a year's time. Both of them obviously heard that word from the angel, talked about and responded to it by having sex in their nineties! They both became doers of the word that was spoken to them. It was God then Who did the impossible inside Sarah's womb. Because of their faith in God to do just exactly what He said, they received potency (dunamis) to conceive a child.

The Japanese character for the word "FAITH" — 信仰 shows a man speaking from his mouth words that God has ordered, commanded or spoken.

Jeremiah 1:7 defines faith the same way, that is "man speaking from his mouth words that God has spoken." *But the Lord said unto me, Say not, I am a child: for thou shalt go to all that I shall send thee, and* **whatsoever I command thee thou shalt speak.**

I Would Not Have You Ignorant

God gave Abraham and Sarah a spoken Promise, words that they both heard and understood. They responded to the word, and their response produced the miracle of Isaac.

Operation of the gift of the working of miracles

First, God prepares a person's heart with a word or thought about the miracle, usually requiring action on the hearer's part for the miracle to come to pass. Secondly, as the person steps out in faith and obeys that word, acting to allow the Holy Spirit to perform it, believing what has been spoken by God will actually happen, then . . . thirdly, the miracle occurs.

One will notice that the gift of faith always seems to accompany the working of miracles and the gift(s) of healing(s). Dick Iverson, the founding pastor of Bible Temple (now City Bible Church), a large charismatic church in Portland, Oregon, says, "Miracles aid the development of faith in the church. The gift of miracles is dependent on the faith and obedience of the believer. The main reason any gift is lacking in the church is because of the lack of faith and obedience."

To those who have been used in the operation of the gifts of the Holy Spirit, when He moves or gives you a word, whether in prophecy, tongues-interpretation, or faith, step out and speak it (obey). It is God who will speak to edify the body of believers present. Lack of faith and obedience can also be called "reluctance" and/or "holding back."

Lastly, Kenneth Hagin relates, "This working of miracles is indeed a mighty gift, glorifying the God of all power, stimulating the faith of His people, astonishing and confusing the unbelief of the world."

POWER GIFT —
The Gift(s) of Healing(s)

We must bring to your attention first that since there are numerous organs operating in our bodies and are prone to sickness and disease, the Holy Spirit has provided numerous gifts(s) of healing(s).

www.howmanyarethere.net states, "There are 78 organs in the human body. There are 13 major organ systems in the human body. The organs work together systematically to keep you alive and active and each plays a specific role related to your health and development."

Here is a list of human internal organs. These do not include the external organs:

Head & Neck — The brain alone has ten organs including the amygdala, basal ganglia, brain stem (medulla, midbrain, pons), cerebellum, cerebral cortex, hypothalamus, and the limbic system. Then there is the eye, pituitary, thyroid, and parathyroids.

Thorax — The heart, lungs, esophagus, thymus, and pleura.

Abdomen and Pelvis — Adrenals, append, bladder, gallbladder, large intestine, small intestine, kidney, liver, pancreas, spleen, and stomach. The male pelvis contains the prostate and testes, while the female pelvis contains the ovaries and uterus.

Plus there are 13 major organ systems listed: circulatory, digestive, endocannabinoid, endocrine, integumentary, immune, lymphatic, musculoskeletal, nervous, reproductive, respiratory, urinary and vestibular systems.

With all these organs and systems in the human body, one can easily understand and see why the Holy Spirit gave "gift(s) of healing(s)" to the Body of Christ. The Apostle John wrote, *Beloved, I wish*

I Would Not Have You Ignorant

above all things that thou mayest prosper and be in health, even as thy soul prospereth. 3 John 1:2

Norvel Hayes, a successful businessman, renowned Bible teacher, and founder of several Christian ministries in the United States and abroad, lists "Seven Ways Jesus Heals" in his book by the same title. God heals —

Through your own faith
Hebrews 11:6; 10:23 *But without faith it is impossible to please him: for he that cometh to God must believe that he is, and that he is a rewarder of them that diligently seek him . . . Let us hold fast the profession of our faith without wavering; (for he is faithful that promised).*

Through laying on of hands
Mark 1:40-41; 16:17-18 *And there came a leper to him, beseeching him, and kneeling down to him, and saying unto him, If thou wilt, thou canst make me clean. And Jesus, moved with compassion, put forth his hand, and touched him, and saith unto him, I will; be thou clean . . . And these signs shall follow them that believe; In my name shall they cast out devils; they shall speak with new tongues; They shall take up serpents; and if they drink any deadly thing, it shall not hurt them; they shall lay hands on the sick, and they shall recover.*

Through the head of the house
Matthew 21:21-22 *Jesus answered and said unto them, Verily I say unto you, If ye have faith, and doubt not, ye shall not only do this which is done to the fig tree, but also if ye shall say unto this mountain, Be thou removed, and be thou cast into the sea; it shall be done. And all things, whatsoever ye shall ask in prayer, believing, ye shall receive.*

God has made the husband the head of the house, in other words, given him authority. So, if the husband has authority, doubts not in that authority and prays, God can heal.

The following is an account of a father in Tokyo (Fussa City), Japan who prayed for his son's healing.

Healing of my son's right leg
by Kuniharu Tanaka

My son, Ryusei started limping on his right leg in early May. When I asked him about it, he reported that he felt pain behind his right knee, and he could not stretch his leg straight.

We decided to wait and see for a while, but it did not improve. So we took him to the clinic in our community. After the examination, we were told by the doctor that our son has a Developmental Disorder, and he had fluid on his knee. The doctor said he will advise us how to deal with the disorder over time.

My wife was devastated, thinking Ryusei will never run again. I was overwhelmed with shock and sorrow.

That day my wife and I sat down and discussed what we to do. We argued because each of us had different opinions.

That night, I placed my hand on Ryusei's right knee and prayed in Jesus' name. I prayed so hard for about an hour, pouring out my hearAs the Word in Psalm 103:3 says, *"He forgives all my sins and heals all my diseases,"* I believed it and claimed that there is no illness in my family and I continued to pray with the Holy Spirit. My son's leg was still the same the next morning, but we sent him to preschool as usual.

Another day passed and we noticed that his leg seemed better.

The doctor told us the developmental disorder had disappeared and the fluid around his knee was reduced. The doctor was confused that the problem had disappeared and he canceled the diagnoses. He said my son now has no problem.

As soon as I heard it, I was convinced that Jesus had listened to our prayers and healed my son with his healing touch.

But we were more surprised when we heard our son say, "I saw God coming down from the sky in my dream, and He asked me if my leg hurts."

When I heard that, I believed that Jesus had healed him completely from the evil of illness.

We give thanks to God. We came here today because we decided to testify of God's mighty healing power. We continue to trust in Him, because He lives. He indeed listens when we pray as the Scripture tells us. We will continue to seek after the Holy Spirit and His Words.

Through the gift(s) of healing(s)
1 Corinthians 12:1, 9 *Now concerning spiritual gifts, brethren, I would not have you ignorant . . . To another faith by the same Spirit; to another the gifts of healing by the same Spirit.*

Through anointing with oil
James 5:14-16 *Is any sick among you? let him call for the elders of the church; and let them pray over him, anointing him with oil in the name of the Lord: And the prayer of faith shall save the sick, and the Lord shall raise him up; and if he have committed sins, they shall be forgiven him. Confess your faults one to another, and pray one for another, that ye may be healed. The effectual fervent prayer of a righteous man availeth much.*

Through special miracles
Acts 9:11-12 *And the Lord said unto him, Arise, and go into the street which is called Straight, and enquire in the house of Judas for one called Saul, of Tarsus: for, behold, he prayeth, And hath seen in a vision a man named Ananias coming in, and putting his hand on him, that he might receive his sight.*

Through praying for others
James 5:16 *Confess your faults one to another, and pray one for another, that ye may be healed. The effectual fervent prayer of a righteous man availeth much.*

According to Kenneth Hagin, "the purpose of the gift(s) of healing(s) is to deliver the sick person and to destroy the works of the devil in the human body." Hagin also relates there are no natural means of healing when this/these gift(s) of healing(s) are operated. "Natural means" include medicines, treatments, doctors and hospital care. Hagen states, "If this was the case, then healing by doctors, medicine, hospital care etc. would be free." Medicine is only temporary.

The Holy Spirit's gift(s) of healing(s) are SUPERNATURAL and are always coupled and operate with His gift of faith. We can see this principle in Matthew 13:58, *And he did not many mighty works there because of their unbelief.*

There are basically two kinds of healing that take place in scripture:

Instantaneous — which can also be classified as miracles. Matthew 8:3, *And Jesus put forth his hand, and touched him, saying, I will; be thou clean. And immediately his leprosy was cleansed.*

Gradual — Mental sickness may be a result of the inner-man being sick or hurt. The soul (emotions), or the spirit of the individual may need to be healed first. This is not necessarily instant, but will rather take time.

A person's heart attitude may need healing before their physical healing takes place. Inner healing gifts may include the operation of the gift of the word of knowledge, and discerning of spirits in order to help deal with these kinds of people.

John 4:43-54 (especially verse 52) *Now after two days he departed thence, and went into Galilee. For Jesus himself testified, that a prophet hath no honour in his own country. Then when he was come into Galilee, the Galilaeans received him, having seen all the things that he did at Jerusalem at the feast: for they also went unto the feast. So Jesus came again into Cana of Galilee, where he made the water wine. And there was a certain nobleman, whose son was sick at Capernaum. When he heard that Jesus was come out of Judaea into Galilee, he went unto him, and besought him that he would come down, and heal his son: for he was at the point of death. Then said Jesus unto him, Except ye see signs and wonders, ye will not believe. The nobleman saith unto him, Sir, come down ere my child die. Jesus saith unto him, Go thy way; thy son liveth. And the man believed the word that Jesus had spoken unto him, and he went his way. And as he was now going down, his servants met him, and told him, saying, Thy son liveth.* **Then enquired he of them the hour when he began to amend. And they said unto him, Yesterday at the seventh hour the fever left him.** *So the father knew that it was at the same hour, in the which Jesus said unto him, Thy son liveth: and himself believed, and his whole house. This is again the second miracle that Jesus did, when he was come out of Judaea into Galilee.*

As the scripture says, there are also probably countless other gradual healings that have taken place since Jesus walked the earth. John 20:30-31, John 21:25 *And many other signs truly did Jesus in the presence of his disciples, which are not written in this book: But these are written, that ye might believe that Jesus is the Christ, the Son of God; and that believing ye might have life through his name . . . And there are also many other things which Jesus did, the which, if they should be written every one, I suppose that even the world itself could not contain the books that should be written. Amen.*

In his book The Holy Spirit Today, Dick Iverson relates that there are several ways one can know if he/she is being used in the gift(s) of healing(s).

— By the inner witness of the Holy Spirit, or by just simply knowing.

— By the ability to believe God for healing. There is no question in your heart that God cannot heal.

— Through compassion for the sick.

Compassion on two blind men. Matthew 20:34 *So Jesus had compassion on them, and touched their eyes: and immediately their eyes received sight, and they followed him.*

Compassion on a leper. Mark 1:41 *And Jesus, moved with compassion, put forth his hand, and touched him, and saith unto him, I will; be thou clean.*

Compassion on a widow. Luke 7:12-14 *Now when he came nigh to the gate of the city, behold, there was a dead man carried out, the only son of his mother, and she was a widow: and much people of the city was with her. And when the Lord saw her, he had compassion on her, and said unto her, Weep not. And he came and touched the bier: and they that bare him stood still. And he said, Young man, I say unto thee, Arise. And he that was dead sat up, and began to speak. And he delivered him to his mother.*

The young man, whose death was probably caused by some

sickness, was raised from the dead by the working of a miracle. We can understand from this that many times giftings of the Holy Spirit work together.

— By results. The test of any ministry gift is the fruit it bears.

— By people recognizing it and by people coming to you for prayer. Proverbs 18:16 *A man's gift maketh room for him, and bringeth him before great men.*

Contrast Proverbs 25:14 where is says, *Whoso boasteth himself of a false gift is like clouds and wind without rain.*

— By laying on of hands of the presbytery. When prophetic ministry establishes a person in his place in the Body of Christ, many times gifts and ministries are clearly spoken.

1 Timothy 1:18; 4:14 *This charge I commit unto thee, son Timothy, according to the prophecies which went before on thee, that thou by them mightest war a good warfare . . . Neglect not the gift that is in thee, which was given thee by prophecy, with the laying on of the hands of the presbytery.*

2 Timothy 1:6 *Wherefore I put thee in remembrance that thou stir up the gift of God, which is in thee by the putting on of my hands.*

Notice what the authorized King James Version states in the verses below regarding the Holy Spirit's "gift of healing." A plurality of gifts of healing is very evident.

1 Corinthians 12:9, 28 and 30 *To another faith by the same Spirit; to another the **gifts of healing** by the same Spirit . . . And God hath set some in the church, first apostles, secondarily prophets, thirdly teachers, after that miracles, then **gifts of healings**, helps, governments, diversities of tongues . . . Have all the **gifts of healing**? do all speak with tongues? do all interpret?*

God knows and wants to heal every kind of sickness. Therefore He has given different gifts of healing to different people in the body of

Christ. Matthew 4:23 says, *And Jesus went about all Galilee, teaching in their synagogues, and preaching the gospel of the kingdom, and **healing all manner of sickness and all manner of disease** among the people.*

The Amplified of Matthew 10:1 says also that *JESUS summoned to Him His twelve disciples and gave them power and authority over unclean spirits, to drive them out, and **to cure all kinds of disease and all kinds of weakness and infirmity**.*

As we bring this section of our study on the Holy Spirit's gifts of healings to a close, we would like you to notice as you read the Gospels that Jesus always taught and preached the Word before practicing what He preached.

It is the Word that heals, and if there is no teaching or preaching of it first, then there will likely be no manifestation of healing.

Psalm 107:19-20 *Then they cry unto the Lord in their trouble, and he saveth them out of their distresses. **He sent his word, and healed them, and delivered them from their destructions.** Oh that men would praise the Lord for his goodness, and for his wonderful works to the children of men.*

Operation of the gift(s) of healing(s)

— A word of faith (i.e. the gift of faith) is spoken by a word of knowledge or the gift of discernment.
— Obedience to that word brings the . . .
— Healing or miracle.

In addition to the teaching in this book, it is very important to realize that healing, whether spiritual, emotional or physical, has its origin in Isaiah 53:4-12.

Surely he hath borne our griefs, and carried our sorrows: yet we did esteem him stricken, smitten of God, and afflicted. But he was wounded for our transgressions, he was bruised for our iniquities:

the chastisement of our peace was upon him; and with his stripes we are healed. All we like sheep have gone astray; we have turned every one to his own way; and the Lord hath laid on him the iniquity of us all. He was oppressed, and he was afflicted, yet he opened not his mouth: he is brought as a lamb to the slaughter, and as a sheep before her shearers is dumb, so he openeth not his mouth. He was taken from prison and from judgment: and who shall declare his generation for he was cut off out of the land of the living: for the transgression of my people was he stricken. And he made his grave with the wicked, and with the rich in his death; because he had done no violence, neither was any deceit in his mouth. Yet it pleased the Lord to bruise him; he hath put him to grief: when thou shalt make his soul an offering for sin, he shall see his seed, he shall prolong his days, and the pleasure of the Lord shall prosper in his hand. He shall see of the travail of his soul, and shall be satisfied: by his knowledge shall my righteous servant justify many; for he shall bear their iniquities. Therefore will I divide him a portion with the great, and he shall divide the spoil with the strong; because he hath poured out his soul unto death: and he was numbered with the transgressors; and he bare the sin of many, and made intercession for the transgressors.

The Apostle Peter also made mention of this Old Testament foundation of healing when he quoted Isaiah in his First Letter 2:20-25.

For what glory is it, if, when ye be buffeted for your faults, ye shall take it patiently? but if, when ye do well, and suffer for it, ye take it patiently, this is acceptable with God. For even hereunto were ye called: because Christ also suffered for us, leaving us an example, that ye should follow his steps: Who did no sin, neither was guile found in his mouth: Who, when he was reviled, reviled not again; when he suffered, he threatened not; but committed himself to him that judgeth righteously: Who his own self bare our sins in his own body on the tree, that we, being dead to sins, should live unto righteousness: **by whose stripes ye were healed**. *For ye were as sheep going astray; but are now returned unto the Shepherd and Bishop of your souls.*

—JESUS bore our illness, disease, even bad habits;
—JESUS carried our aches and pains;
—JESUS was pierced for our national, moral and religious rebellion;
—JESUS was beaten, crushed, destroyed for our moral evil.
—JESUS' punishment brought us our peace.
—JESUS' stripes, bruises, blue marks healed us all.

Make JESUS the Lord of your heart and healing begins! Healing of your spirit, soul, and body: healing for your whole man.

1 Thessalonians 5:23-24 *And the very God of peace sanctify you wholly; and I pray God your whole spirit and soul and body be preserved blameless unto the coming of our Lord Jesus Christ. Faithful is he that calleth you, who also will do it.*

REVELATION GIFT — The Word of Wisdom

Kenneth Hagin emphasizes, "It is NOT the **gift of wisdom.** It is the **word of wisdom.** God knows all things but never reveals all. He rather gives A WORD of what He knows. If we had the gift of wisdom, we would have ALL wisdom. The same is emphasized for the gift of knowledge. It is NOT the gift, but rather A WORD. If we had knowledge and wisdom in gift form, we would have no need to know anything."

There is a difference between the word of wisdom and the word of knowledge. The **WORD OF WISDOM** is a supernatural revelation by the Holy Spirit about the purpose and plan in the mind and will of God. It speaks of the **FUTURE**. While on the other hand, the **WORD OF KNOWLEDGE** is a supernatural revelation by the Holy Spirit about facts in the mind of God concerning people, places or things. It ALWAYS speaks of things **PAST or PRESENT**. One cannot be knowledgeable of the future; he can only know of things past or present.

The word of wisdom is NOT natural wisdom. It is supernatural.

I Would Not Have You Ignorant

Natural wisdom is given to all men to deal in the affairs of everyday life.

James 1:5 *If any of you lack wisdom, let him ask of God, that giveth to ALL MEN liberally, and upbraideth not; and it shall be given him.*

The Greek word for 'wisdom' is σοφία 'sophia,' meaning higher or lower, worldly or spiritual wisdom. This definition shows that there are two kinds of wisdom. All people can have general wisdom for the affairs of everyday life, BUT . . . 1 Corinthians 12:8 says, *For to ONE is given by the Spirit the word of wisdom.*

The LORD spoke to Joshua and said, *This book of the law shall not depart out of thy mouth; but thou shalt meditate therein day and night, that thou mayest observe to do according to all that is written therein: for then thou shalt make thy way prosperous, and then thou shalt have **good success**.* Joshua 1:8

"Good success" here means **"to do wisely."** Wisdom to live our Christian lives is given to us as we read, study, meditate on and practice the Word of God.

Proverbs 2:10-17 *When **wisdom entereth into thine heart**, and knowledge is pleasant unto thy soul; Discretion shall preserve thee, understanding shall keep thee: To deliver thee from the way of the evil man, from the man that speaketh froward things; Who leave the paths of uprightness, to walk in the ways of darkness; Who rejoice to do evil, and delight in the frowardness of the wicked; Whose ways are crooked, and they froward in their paths: To deliver thee from the strange woman, even from the stranger which flattereth with her words; Which forsaketh the guide of her youth, and forgetteth the covenant of her God.*

The Holy Spirit's Word of Wisdom is made known in several different ways. I may be:

—The audible voice of God.
Moses received the Law by the audible voice of God. In bold type

below, we can clearly see a Word of Wisdom speaking of something in future.

Exodus 19:1-7 *In the third month, when the children of Israel were gone forth out of the land of Egypt, the same day came they into the wilderness of Sinai. For they were departed from Rephidim, and were come to the desert of Sinai, and had pitched in the wilderness; and there Israel camped before the mount. And Moses went up unto God, and the Lord called unto him out of the mountain, saying, Thus shalt thou say to the house of Jacob, and tell the children of Israel; Ye have seen what I did unto the Egyptians, and how I bare you on eagles' wings, and brought you unto myself.* **Now therefore, if ye will obey my voice indeed, and keep my covenant, then ye shall be a peculiar treasure unto me above all people: for all the earth is mine: And ye shall be unto me a kingdom of priests, and an holy nation. These are the words which thou shalt speak unto the children of Israel.** *And Moses came and called for the elders of the people, and laid before their faces all these words which the Lord commanded him.*

—A vision.
Acts 16:9-10 (Gospel to Macedonia) *And a vision appeared to Paul in the night; There stood a man of Macedonia, and prayed him, saying, Come over into Macedonia, and help us. 10 And after he had seen* **the vision**, *immediately we endeavoured to go into Macedonia, assuredly gathering that the Lord had called us for to preach the gospel unto them.*

Acts 18:7-11 (Pioneering the Corinthian church) *And he departed thence, and entered into a certain man's house, named Justus, one that worshipped God, whose house joined hard to the synagogue. 8 And Crispus, the chief ruler of the synagogue, believed on the Lord with all his house; and many of the Corinthians hearing believed, and were baptized. 9 Then spake the Lord to Paul in the night by* **a vision**, *Be not afraid, but speak, and hold not thy peace: 10 For I am with thee, and no man shall set on thee to hurt thee: for I have much people in this city. 11 And he continued there a year and six months, teaching the word of God among them.*
Acts 27:10, 22-25 (Paul on his way to Rome) *And said unto them,*

Sirs, I perceive that this voyage will be with hurt and much damage, not only of the lading and ship, but also of our lives . . . And now I exhort you to be of good cheer: for there shall be no loss of any man's life among you, but of the ship. **For there stood by me this night the angel of God**, *whose I am, and whom I serve,* **Saying**, *Fear not, Paul; thou must be brought before Caesar: and, lo, God hath given thee all them that sail with thee. Wherefore, sirs, be of good cheer: for I believe God, that it shall be even as it was told me.*

—A dream.
Genesis 37:5-11 (Joseph's dreams) *And Joseph dreamed a dream, and he told it his brethren: and they hated him yet the more. And he said unto them, Hear, I pray you, this dream which I have dreamed: For, behold, we were binding sheaves in the field, and, lo, my sheaf arose, and also stood upright; and, behold, your sheaves stood round about, and made obeisance to my sheaf. And his brethren said to him, Shalt thou indeed reign over us? or shalt thou indeed have dominion over us? And they hated him yet the more for his dreams, and for his words. And he dreamed yet another dream, and told it his brethren, and said, Behold, I have dreamed a dream more; and, behold, the sun and the moon and the eleven stars made obeisance to me. And he told it to his father, and to his brethren: and his father rebuked him, and said unto him, What is this dream that thou hast dreamed? Shall I and thy mother and thy brethren indeed come to bow down ourselves to thee to the earth? And his brethren envied him; but his father observed the saying.*

—The vocal gift of prophecy.
Acts 11:27-30 (Future famine) *And in these days came prophets from Jerusalem unto Antioch. And there stood up one of them named Agabus, and signified by the Spirit that there should be great dearth throughout all the world: which came to pass in the days of Claudius Caesar. Then the disciples, every man according to his ability, determined to send relief unto the brethren which dwelt in Judaea: Which also they did, and sent it to the elders by the hands of Barnabas and Saul.*

Acts 21:10-14 (Paul's future) *And as we tarried there many days, there came down from Judaea a certain prophet, named Agabus.*

And when he was come unto us, he took Paul's girdle, and bound his own hands and feet, and said, Thus saith the Holy Ghost, So shall the Jews at Jerusalem bind the man that owneth this girdle, and shall deliver him into the hands of the Gentiles. And when we heard these things, both we, and they of that place, besought him not to go up to Jerusalem. Then Paul answered, What mean ye to weep and to break mine heart? for I am ready not to be bound only, but also to die at Jerusalem for the name of the Lord Jesus. And when he would not be persuaded, we ceased, saying, The will of the Lord be done.

Acts 23:10-11 tells us of the fulfillment of that word. *And when there arose a great dissension, the chief captain, fearing lest Paul should have been pulled in pieces of them, commanded the soldiers to go down, and to take him by force from among them, and to bring him into the castle. And the night following the Lord stood by him, and said, Be of good cheer, Paul: for as thou hast testified of me in Jerusalem, so must thou bear witness also at Rome.*

—**Tongues and interpretation**, because they are equal to prophecy.

—**The Word of Wisdom and the Word of Knowledge** because they often work together.

Acts 9:10-16 *And there was a certain disciple at Damascus, named Ananias; and to him said the Lord* **in a vision**, *Ananias. And he said, Behold, I am here, Lord.* **And the Lord said unto him, Arise, and go into the street which is called Straight, and enquire in the house of Judas for one called Saul, of Tarsus: for, behold, he prayeth, And hath seen in a vision a man named Ananias coming in, and putting his hand on him, that he might receive his sight.** *Then Ananias answered, Lord, I have heard by many of this man, how much evil he hath done to thy saints at Jerusalem: And here he hath authority from the chief priests to bind all that call on thy name.* **But the Lord said unto him, Go thy way: for he is a chosen vessel unto me, to bear my name before the Gentiles, and kings, and the children of Israel: For I will shew him how great things he must suffer for my name's sake.**

Notice the vehicle of this Word of Wisdom was a VISION. Verses

11-12 are a Word of Knowledge, but verses 15-16 are a Word of Wisdom revealing the plan and purpose of God concerning Paul. The Word of Knowledge revealed present facts about Paul (where he was and what he was doing), but the Word of Wisdom revealed a future aspect of Paul's ministry to the Gentiles.

Respected teachers of God's Word have said of this revelation gift:

"This gift cannot be gained through study and experience, yet neither is it a substitute for study and experience." —Dick Iverson

"Knowledge and wisdom look and operate much alike, but can be differentiated by past-present and future." —Kenneth Hagin

"This Christ in whom are hid ALL the treasures of wisdom and knowledge." —Paul to the Colossians

These two revelation gifts are given to the church for a reason: so we won't be in the dark! *But as it is written, Eye hath not seen, nor ear heard, neither have entered into the heart of man, the things which God hath prepared for them that love him. But God hath revealed them unto us by his Spirit: for the Spirit searcheth all things, yea, the deep things of God. For what man knoweth the things of a man, save the spirit of man which is in him? even so the things of God knoweth no man, but the Spirit of God. Now we have received, not the spirit of the world, but the spirit which is of God; that we might know the things that are freely given to us of God.* —Paul to the Corinthians

REVELATION GIFT — The Word of Knowledge

As in the word of wisdom, so it is a WORD of knowledge. If it was the gift of knowledge, we would know all things and have no need of education, studying, or investigating. Only God can know all things because He is almighty. God's knowledge of us is unthinkable and mind-boggling!

O Lord, thou hast searched me, and known me. Thou knowest my downsitting and mine uprising, thou understandest my thought afar off. Thou compassest my path and my lying down, and art acquainted with all my ways. For there is not a word in my tongue, but, lo, O Lord, thou knowest it altogether. Thou hast beset me behind and before, and laid thine hand upon me. Such knowledge is too wonderful for me; it is high, I cannot attain unto it . . . Search me, O God, and know my heart: try me, and know my thoughts: And see if there be any wicked way in me, and lead me in the way everlasting. Psalm 139:1-6, 23-24

The Holy Spirit gives us knowledge about God as we read, study, and pray. One's level of knowledge about God depends on his/her relationship and how much time he/she spends with Him. For example, one might ask, "How well do I know my husband or wife?"

If ye love me, keep my commandments. And I will pray the Father, and he shall give you another Comforter, that he may abide with you for ever; Even the Spirit of truth; whom the world cannot receive, because it seeth him not, neither knoweth him: but ye know him; for he dwelleth with you, and shall be in you. I will not leave you comfortless: I will come to you . . . But the Comforter, which is the Holy Ghost, whom the Father will send in my name, he shall teach you all things, and bring all things to your remembrance, whatsoever I have said unto you. John 14:15-18, 26

But the anointing which ye have received of him abideth in you, and ye need not that any man teach you: but as the same anointing teacheth you of all things, and is truth, and is no lie, and even as it hath taught you, ye shall abide in him. 1 John 2:27

But grow in grace, and in the knowledge of our Lord and Saviour Jesus Christ. To him be glory both now and for ever. Amen. 2 Peter 3:18

There are different types of knowledge. For instance, there is a tendency to acquire knowledge by studying, researching and deeply reflecting on something that interests a person. How many years does one spend gaining enough knowledge to graduate from an institution of higher learning, and then pursue an adult life? In fact, do we not find ourselves becoming knowledgeable of things around us until the day we die?

There is also a general knowledge of people, places, things, and dates to which we all have access. Google something, and, poof, it appears before your eyes in the wink of an eye.

How about an intimate knowledge of the ones with whom we live, work and play? The more time spent with one's husband, wife, and children, or with friends the stronger a relationship becomes. The more time spent with God Himself and His Word will result in a strong, immovable, and mature relationship.

This gift of the word for knowledge is the supernatural revelation by the Holy Spirit of certain facts in the mind of God Himself and can be made known in many different ways.

—Visions

I was in the Spirit on the Lord's day, and heard behind me a great voice, as of a trumpet . . . Revelation 1:10

John, in the Spirit, or by the Spirit, saw the conditions of the seven churches in Asia Minor. He was in exile at the time, so he could not have possibly known those conditions. The Holy Spirit revealed them to him by a word of knowledge.

Ananias was given a word of knowledge about Paul by the Spirit in a vision during prayer; where and in what condition he was.

And there was a certain disciple at Damascus, named Ananias; and to him said the Lord in a vision, Ananias. And he said, Behold, I am here, Lord. And the Lord said unto him, Arise, and go into the street which is called Straight, and enquire in the house of Judas for one called Saul, of Tarsus: for, behold, he prayeth, And hath seen in a vision a man named Ananias coming in, and putting his hand on him, that he might receive his sight. Acts 9:10-12

Peter, at a time of prayer, saw in a vision the plan of God for the Gentile world. That was a word of wisdom. But verses 19-20 show the Holy Spirit giving specific knowledge that men were looking for him. Notice also where Cornelius saw in a vision and received specific knowledge of where Peter could be found.

9 On the morrow, as they went on their journey, and drew nigh unto the city, Peter went up upon the housetop to pray about the sixth hour: 10 And he became very hungry, and would have eaten: but while they made ready, he fell into a trance, 11 And saw heaven opened, and a certain vessel descending unto him, as it had been a great sheet knit at the four corners, and let down to the earth: 12 Wherein were all manner of fourfooted beasts of the earth, and wild beasts, and creeping things, and fowls of the air. 13 And there came a voice to him, Rise, Peter; kill, and eat. 14 But Peter said, Not so, Lord; for I have never eaten any thing that is common or unclean. 15 And the voice spake unto him again the second time, What God hath cleansed, that call not thou common. 16 This was done thrice: and the vessel was received up again into heaven. 17 Now while Peter doubted in himself what this vision which he had seen should mean, behold, the men which were sent from Cornelius had made enquiry for Simon's house, and stood before the gate, 18 And called, and asked whether Simon, which was surnamed Peter, were lodged there. 19 While Peter thought on the vision, the Spirit said unto him, Behold, three men seek thee. 20 Arise therefore, and get thee down, and go with them, doubting nothing: for I have sent them. Acts 10:9-20

Notice also how Cornelius saw in a vision and received specific knowledge of where Peter could be found.

There was a certain man in Caesarea called Cornelius, a centurion of the band called the Italian band, A devout man, and one that feared God with all his house, which gave much alms to the people, and prayed to God alway. He saw in a vision evidently about the ninth hour of the day an angel of God coming in to him, and saying unto him, Cornelius. And when he looked on him, he was afraid, and said, What is it, Lord? And he said unto him, Thy prayers and thine alms are come up for a memorial before God. And now send men to

Joppa, and call for one Simon, whose surname is Peter: He lodgeth with one Simon a tanner, whose house is by the sea side: he shall tell thee what thou oughtest to do. And when the angel which spake unto Cornelius was departed, he called two of his household servants, and a devout soldier of them that waited on him continually; And when he had declared all these things unto them, he sent them to Joppa. Acts 10:1-8

—Inward revelations
The woman at the well — The word of knowledge came to Jesus as He was talking to her. This word revealed intimate details of the woman's life-style. The word of knowledge should lead to a person's salvation, healing or deliverance, as in the case of this woman. Results should always occur when this word is operated.

The woman saith unto him, Sir, give me this water, that I thirst not, neither come hither to draw. Jesus saith unto her, Go, call thy husband, and come hither. The woman answered and said, I have no husband. Jesus said unto her, Thou hast well said, I have no husband: For thou hast had five husbands; and he whom thou now hast is not thy husband: in that saidst thou truly. John 4:15-18

The word of knowledge may also manifest in the church by prophecy, tongues, and interpretation, or even an angel-messenger. There are several other scriptures that reveal a word of knowledge. Let's read them together.

He saith unto them, But whom say ye that I am? And Simon Peter answered and said, Thou art the Christ, the Son of the living God. And Jesus answered and said unto him, Blessed art thou, Simon Barjona: for flesh and blood hath not revealed it unto thee, but my Father which is in heaven. Matthew 16:15-17. It was revealed to Peter that Jesus was the Messiah (Christ) by divine revelation.

Acts 5:1-11. Peter KNEW the condition of the hearts of Ananias and Sapphira by revelation. *But a certain man named Ananias, with Sapphira his wife, sold a possession, 2 And kept back part of the price, his wife also being privy to it, and brought a certain part, and laid it at the apostles' feet. 3 But Peter said, Ananias, why hath Satan filled thine heart to lie to the Holy Ghost, and to keep back part of the price of the land? 4 Whilst it remained, was it not thine own? and after it was sold, was it not in thine own power? why hast thou conceived this thing in thine heart? thou hast not lied unto men, but unto God. 5 And Ananias hearing these words fell down, and gave up the ghost: and great fear came on all them that heard these things. 6 And the young men arose, wound him up, and carried him out, and buried him. 7 And it was about the space of three hours after, when his wife, not knowing what was done, came in. 8 And Peter answered unto her, Tell me whether ye sold the land for so much? And she said, Yea, for so much. 9 Then Peter said unto her, How is it that ye have agreed together to tempt the Spirit of the Lord? behold, the feet of them which have buried thy husband are at the door, and shall carry thee out. 10 Then fell she down straightway at his feet, and yielded up the ghost: and the young men came in, and found her dead, and, carrying her forth, buried her by her husband. 11 And great fear came upon all the church, and upon as many as heard these things.*

Acts 18:9-10 reveals certain knowledge concerning Paul's ministry at Corinth. *Then spake the Lord to Paul in the night by a vision, Be not afraid, but speak, and hold not thy peace: For I am with thee, and no man shall set on thee to hurt thee: for I have much people in this city.*

Acts 20:29-31. Paul KNEW about false prophets at Ephesus. *For I know this, that after my departing shall grievous wolves enter in among you, not sparing the flock. Also of your own selves shall men arise, speaking perverse things, to draw away disciples after them. Therefore watch, and remember, that by the space of three years I ceased not to warn every one night and day with tears.*

Acts 27:23-24. Paul KNEW about the safety of their journey on the boat. *For there stood by me this night the angel of God, whose I am, and whom I serve, Saying, Fear not, Paul; thou must be brought before Caesar: and, lo, God hath given thee all them that sail with thee.*

" . . . he that hath an ear, let him hear what the Spirit saith to the

I Would Not Have You Ignorant

churches." This statement is made several times in the Book of Revelation. The content of these vocal "word gifts" determines whether it is a word of wisdom or a word of knowledge. We must learn to train our EARS and listen to each prophecy, tongue, and interpretation to determine whether or not it is a
word of wisdom or a word of knowledge.

There are some important things we should remember about the words of wisdom and knowledge:

—Past-Present is revealed by the word of knowledge.
—Future is revealed by the word of wisdom.
—The word of wisdom and the word of knowledge and sometimes the discerning of spirits operate together, or at the same time.
—Dick Iverson suggests some points to remember when operating in the word of knowledge. He says, "Sometimes when God reveals something by a word of knowledge, it should not necessarily be spoken immediately to the corporate body. If that word comes by a dream or vision, the person receiving it should pray and ask God what to do with it before speaking it forth."

He goes on to relate, "If one receives a word of knowledge about an important situation and does not know what to do with it, he should then consult the pastor/eldership for wisdom in what to do."

Finally, Iverson says, "A word of knowledge may come in a meeting through prophecy. It may be a warning or caution to someone whom God knows is living in sin, or is about to make a major mistake. Of the people who are gathered at the meeting, only the person to whom the word is being spoken will know . . . A word of knowledge can give a person direction or specific guidance in making decisions."

—Knowledge of God and His Word comes via studying and praying, but is NOT the "word of knowledge."

2 Timothy 2:15. *Study to shew thyself approved unto God, a workman that needeth not to be ashamed, rightly dividing the word of truth.*

Acts 17:10-11. And the brethren immediately sent away Paul and Silas by night unto Berea: who coming thither went into the synagogue of the Jews. 11 These were more noble than those in Thessalonica, in that they received the word with all readiness of mind, and searched the scriptures daily, whether those things were so.

Acts 6:4. *But we will give ourselves continually to prayer, and to the ministry of the word.*

Hosea 4:6. *My people are destroyed for lack of knowledge: because thou hast rejected knowledge, I will also reject thee, that thou shalt be no priest to me: seeing thou hast forgotten the law of thy God, I will also forget thy children.*

Extra insight

Except for brief quotes, it is not often that a writer includes a section in his book by another author. However, I would like to include here some personal notes shared by Jeff Earlywine, pastor of Bible Fellowship in Federal Way, Washington. Jeff has been used by the Holy Spirit many times in the operation of this necessary gift to the church.

In 1 Corinthians 12 Paul talks about the gifts of the Spirit. He calls one the "message of knowledge" in the NIV of 1 Corinthians 12:7-8 *Now to each one the manifestation of the Spirit is given for the common good. To one there is given through the Spirit a message of wisdom, to another a message of knowledge by means of the same Spirit . . .*

A word of knowledge is a supernatural revelation of information that is given by the Holy Spirit. It is not something that the person who receives the word knew prior to the meeting or by their own carnal or natural ability or senses. A word of knowledge is supernatural, one revealed to a person by the Holy Spirit. So, in order for it to be by the Spirit, the word must be supernaturally revealed. This means it would have to be information of which one were totally unaware.

I Would Not Have You Ignorant

I can still remember the very first time I was impacted by Holy Spirit speaking to me with a word of knowledge. I had been seeking the Lord spending hours in prayer and focusing on the Holy Spirit during my prayer time. One morning while getting up for a Sunday meeting, I was taken by surprise when the word "foot" kept going over and over in my thinking. I remember asking the Lord, "Why am I thinking the word foot?" Then I suddenly realized the Holy Spirit was giving me that for which I had been seeking and praying. I immediately began thanking Him for the word; I knew it was a word of knowledge but for whom?

I will say right here that many times you'll get a word of knowledge and not know for whom it is, and that's where faith comes in. That morning as I entered the service, I had told the Lord, "OK, if You will remind me of this word I will get it. As we called people up for prayer and ministered to many people and saw healings and saw hearts touched by the Holy Spirit, I was getting ready to move on to another portion of the meeting. When suddenly the Holy Spirit spoke to me again, "Foot, foot." I knew then that I had to give it, so with boldness I put the microphone to my lips and asked, "Who is it that needs healing in their foot?"

Earlier that morning I said to the Lord I would give the word, but I asked Him, "Which foot? Right or left?" He said very clearly, "Right foot!" Then I said, "Okay, black, brown, or colored shoe?" He said again clearly, "Black?" I said, "Okay." "Man or woman?" He replied, "Woman."

Remembering this conversation with Holy Spirit, I wasn't sure who it was, only that it was a word of knowledge. Suddenly, A lady walking past me to head to her seat stopped and said, "Oh my God Jeff, that's me!" I laughed and said let's pray for this then. Her situation was that she needed a surgery for a problem that would not go away unless she had this operation.

Needless to say, God healed her instantly and she went back to her doctor and told him, "JESUS healed my foot, I won't be needing that surgery anymore."

FEEL IT

One of the ways the Holy Spirit speaks to us a word of knowledge is that we feel it. The word will come as a shooting pain, a dull pain, or a brief pain in your body. It is not a pain that you would normally have on your own.

One Sunday morning service I suddenly got a sharp pain in my neck. (No, it was not my wife, my kids or my brother!) It was a sharp pain in my neck for a brief moment and immediately I knew it wasn't mine. I was so excited I could not wait to get to that part of the meeting where I could call this out and see who is about to get healed. As I called it out, a young boy and an older man stood up. I asked people to place their hands on them and we spoke to the pain and told it to go immediately. Then I told the man's body to be made whole in the name of Jesus. The older man said that the pain left as soon as we prayed! Praise God!

READ IT

Another way one may receive a word of knowledge is that one may literally see the words spelled out. Sometimes the words can be seen on the people. For others, it's like a ticker-tape as they read the words passing along. These people actually read the word of knowledge as it passing in front of them. I have never experienced this to that degree, but I have seen men do this.

SEE IT

One experiencing this operation of the Holy Spirit may not see words, but rather a picture in the mind, or imagination.

I have experienced this a few times. I remember one time in Bible study and we were praying for people. Suddenly I saw dark clouds and heard the Lord say, "Nightmares." When the time was right I spoke up and asked,"Who is having nightmares? I see dark clouds in the night and the word nightmares." A few hands went up in the room and we began to pray for each one. This is also how it happened in Japan once when I saw the word "Uncommon Favor" above a young man and I knew God was imparting the supernatural favor of the Holy Spirit.

THINK IT
This is where the thoughts just flash into your mind, like when I woke up in the morning and heard in my thoughts the word "foot". Many times people will get bank numbers or birthday dates and so on. Many times these are things no other person would know. But JESUS knows everything and He will often do this just to let you know He is with you and He loves you.

SAY IT
Another way to receive words of knowledge is what is called "inspired speech." This comes suddenly or abruptly while you're praying or talking with someone. Many times you can speak a word of knowledge and then say to yourself, "Why did I say that?" This happened to us in a Bible study one week on a Sunday night. While we were all praying for each other someone had led out in prayer and said, "Lord just send somebody by tomorrow to give Pastor the money he needs to pay for rent." That was actually a word of knowledge. Earlier in the meeting, I had been asking the Lord how He was going to provide my finances. Then suddenly this inspired prayer. I just knew God had provided yet I hadn't seen it in the natural yet. I got excited and began thanking the Lord for His abundant supply. So, when the prayer was given, the person may not have known but I did, it was a word of knowledge to me. Praise God! The next morning someone pulled up and gave us the exact amount of money we needed to pay the rent and drove off. God is so good to us and loves to tells us what He is going to do before He even does it. It is up to us to "see" it in the spirit realm first, then watch God supply and move it into the physical.

DREAM IT
Sometimes one will get a very vivid and detailed dream. Then later you will experience what was in that dream, all the details of what was happening and what God is telling you to do. This is when the Holy Spirit speaks to you in your sleep and you can retain all the information given to you.

REVELATION GIFT — The Discerning of Spirits

The definition of "discern" is to tell or distinguish. Also implied in the meaning is "seeing." Another phrase used to explain the idea of "discern" is to separate thoroughly.

GOD is a Spirit and His entire world [realm] is a spirit realm. John 4:24 states, *"God is a SPIRIT: and they that worship Him must worship Him in spirit* [realm] *and in truth."* [realm] added by author.

Hebrews 12:9. God is the Father of spirits. *Furthermore we have had fathers of our flesh which corrected us, and we gave them reverence: shall we not much rather be in subjection unto the Father of spirits, and live?*

Hebrews 1:7, 14. Angels are spirit beings. *And of the angels he saith, Who maketh his angels spirits, and his ministers a flame of fire . . . Are they not all ministering spirits, sent forth to minister for them who shall be heirs of salvation?*

Genesis 3:24. Cherubim are spirit beings. They are for protection. *So he* (the LORD God) *drove out the man; and he placed at the east of the garden of Eden Cherubims, and a flaming sword which turned every way, to keep the way of the tree of life.*

Isaiah 6:2-6. Seraphim are spirit beings for glorifying God. *Above it stood the seraphims: each one had six wings; with twain he covered his face, and with twain he covered his feet, and with twain he did fly. And one cried unto another, and said, Holy, holy, holy, is the LORD of hosts: the whole earth is full of his glory. And the posts of the door moved at the voice of him that cried, and the house was filled with smoke. Then said I, Woe is me! for I am undone; because I am a man of unclean lips, and I dwell in the midst of a people of unclean lips: for mine eyes have seen the King, the LORD of hosts. Then flew one of the seraphims unto me, having a live coal in his*

hand, which he had taken with the tongs from off the altar.
Daniel 7:10. Spirit beings cannot be numbered.
A fiery stream issued and came forth from before him: thousand thousands ministered unto him, and ten thousand times ten thousand stood before him: the judgment was set, and the books were opened.

Matthew 26:53. Twelve legions (72,000) of angels. *Thinkest thou that I cannot now pray to my Father, and he shall presently give me more than twelve legions of angels?*

1 Samuel 1:3. God is the "LORD of hosts." This word in Hebrew (tsaw-baw) means a mass of persons especially (an army) organized for war. *And this man went up out of his city yearly to worship and to sacrifice unto the LORD of hosts in Shiloh. And the two sons of Eli, Hophni and Phinehas, the priests of the LORD, were there.*

Romans 8:31 points out clearly, *What shall we then say to these things? If God be for us, who can be against us?*

MAN is created in God's image. Man is a spirit being living in a body of flesh. Or, as Dick Iverson says, "Man is a soul and a spirit clothed with flesh."

Genesis 1:26-27. *And God said, Let us make man in our image, after our likeness: and let them have dominion over the fish of the sea, and over the fowl of the air, and over the cattle, and over all the earth, and over every creeping thing that creepeth upon the earth. So God created man in his own image, in the image of God created he him; male and female created he them.*

Genesis 2:7. *And the LORD God formed man of the dust of the ground, and breathed into his nostrils the breath* (spirit) *of life; and man became a living soul.*

It is worthy to also note what Job, Zechariah, Paul and James mention in these scriptures.

Job 32:8. *But there is a spirit in man: and the inspiration of the Almighty giveth them understanding.*

Job 33.4. *The Spirit of God hath made me, and the breath of the Almighty hath given me life.* The Japanese character used for the word "breath" in this scripture is "iki" 息 and shows God breathing into man's nostrils His own heart.

Zechariah 12:1. *The burden of the word of the LORD for Israel, saith the LORD, which stretcheth forth the heavens, and layeth the foundation of the earth, and formeth the spirit of man within him.*

1 Corinthians 2:11. *For what man knoweth the things of a man, save the spirit of man which is in him? even so the things of God knoweth no man, but the Spirit of God.*

James 2:26. *For as the body without the spirit is dead, so faith without works is dead also.*

SATAN is also a spirit being. The prophets Isaiah and Ezekiel tell us that he fell from a high angelic position because of pride, ambition and rebellion.

Isaiah 14:12-15. *How art thou fallen from heaven, O Lucifer, son of the morning! how art thou cut down to the ground, which didst weaken the nations! 13 For thou hast said in thine heart, I will ascend into heaven, I will exalt my throne above the stars of God: I will sit also upon the mount of the congregation, in the sides of the north: 14 I will ascend above the heights of the clouds; I will be like the most High. 15 Yet thou shalt be brought down to hell, to the sides of the pit.*

Ezekiel 28:12-18. *Son of man, take up a lamentation upon the king of Tyrus, and say unto him, Thus saith the Lord God; Thou sealest up the sum, full of wisdom, and perfect in beauty. 13 Thou hast been in Eden the garden of God; every precious stone was thy covering, the sardius, topaz, and the diamond, the beryl, the onyx, and the jasper, the sapphire, the emerald, and the carbuncle, and gold: the workmanship of thy tabrets and of thy pipes was prepared in thee in the day that thou wast created. 14 Thou art the anointed cherub that covereth; and I have set thee so: thou wast upon the holy mountain of God; thou hast walked up and down in the midst of the stones of fire. 15 Thou wast perfect in thy ways from the day that thou wast created, till iniquity was found in thee. 16 By the multitude of thy merchandise they have filled the midst of thee with violence, and thou hast sinned: therefore I will cast thee as profane out of the mountain of God: and I will destroy thee, O covering cherub, from the midst of the stones of fire. 17 Thine heart was lifted up because of thy beauty, thou hast corrupted thy wisdom by reason of thy brightness: I will cast thee to the ground, I will lay thee before kings, that they may behold thee. 18 Thou hast defiled thy sanctuaries by the multitude of thine iniquities, by the iniquity of thy traffick; therefore will I bring forth a fire from the midst of thee, it shall devour thee, and I will bring thee to ashes upon the earth in the sight of all them that behold thee.*

Lucifer, who became SATAN, the arch enemy of Almighty God, defined by dictionary.com as the chief evil spirit, and the great adversary of humanity, took with him a HOST of angelic (spirit) beings. We call them "evil" or "demon" spirits, also "devils." Matthew, Peter, and Jude speak of the plummet of these spirit beings from the kingdom of light into the realm of darkness.

Matthew 25:41. *Then shall he say also unto them on the left hand, Depart from me, ye cursed, into everlasting fire, prepared for the devil and his angels:*

2 Peter 2:4. *For if God spared not the angels that sinned, but cast them down to hell, and delivered them into chains of darkness, to be reserved unto judgment . . .*

Jude 6. *And the angels which kept not their first estate, but left their own habitation, he hath reserved in everlasting chains under darkness unto the judgment of the great day.*

The Amplified says, *And ANGELS that did not keep (care for, guard and hold to) their own first place of power but abandoned their proper dwelling place, He has reserved in custody in eternal chains (bonds) under the thick gloom of utter darkness until the judgment and doom of the great day.*

There are many other scriptures that describe the world (realm) of evil spirits in great detail.

Matthew 12:43-45. **Unclean spirits seek places to live.**
When the unclean spirit is gone out of a man, he walketh through dry places, seeking rest, and findeth none. 44 Then he saith, I will return into my house from whence I came out; and when he is come, he findeth it empty, swept, and garnished. 45 Then goeth he, and taketh with himself seven other spirits more wicked than himself, and they enter in and dwell there: and the last state of that man is worse than the first. Even so shall it be also unto this wicked generation.

Luke 10:17-20. **Spirits are subject unto us.**
And the seventy returned again with joy, saying, Lord, even the devils are subject unto us through thy name. 18 And he said unto them, I beheld Satan as lightning fall from heaven. 19 Behold, I give unto you power to tread on serpents and scorpions, and over all the power of the enemy: and nothing shall by any means hurt you. 20 Notwithstanding in this rejoice not, that the spirits are subject unto you; but rather rejoice, because your names are written in heaven.

1 Timothy 4:1. **Seducing spirits; doctrines of devils.**
Now the Spirit speaketh expressly, that in the latter times some shall depart from the faith, giving heed to seducing spirits, and doctrines of devils . . .

Revelation 16:13-14. **Devils working miracles.**
And I saw three unclean spirits like frogs come out of the mouth of the dragon, and out of the mouth of the beast, and out of the mouth of the false prophet. 14 For they are the spirits of devils, working miracles, which go forth unto the kings of the earth and of the whole world, to gather them to the battle of that great day of God Almighty.

We have seen that there are only three kinds of spirit beings: God, man and Satan — and we find that it is we who are sandwiched right smack in the middle. As Paul said to Timothy, "seducing spirits and doctrines of devils" will increase as we near the end. Therefore, it is vitally important that local church leadership needs the ability to distinguish between the activities and manifestations that these three spirits that may reveal in church-related affairs, including a church service.

We are instructed to "try the spirits" (plural) whether they are of God.

1 John 4:1-4. *Beloved, believe not every spirit, but try the spirits whether they are of God: because many false prophets are gone out into the world. 2 Hereby know ye the Spirit of God: Every spirit that confesseth that Jesus Christ is come in the flesh is of God: 3 And every spirit that confesseth not that Jesus Christ is come in the flesh is not of God: and this is that spirit of antichrist, whereof ye have heard that it should come; and even now already is it in the world. 4 Ye are of God, little children, and have overcome them: because greater is he that is in you, than he that is in the world.*

Note especially verse 3, *And every spirit that confesseth not that Jesus Christ is come in the flesh is not of God: and this is that spirit of antichrist.* The expression 'come in the flesh' is indicative of the birth, death, burial, resurrection of Jesus, as the promised Messiah, and the manifestation of the resurrection power of the Holy Spirit. Paul defines these important points as "the gospel" in 1 Corinthians 15:1-8. Note bold print.

Moreover, brethren, I declare unto you **the gospel** *which I preached unto you, which also ye have received, and wherein ye stand; 2 By which also ye are saved, if ye keep in memory what I preached unto you, unless ye have believed in vain. 3 For I delivered unto you first of all that which I also received, how that* **Christ died for our sins** *according to the scriptures; 4 And that* **he was buried**, *and that* **he rose again** *the third day according to the scriptures: 5 And that* **he was seen** *of Cephas, then of the twelve: 6 After that,* **he was seen** *of above five hundred brethren at once; of whom the greater part remain unto this present, but some are fallen asleep. 7 After that,* **he was seen** *of James; then of all the apostles. 8 And last of all* **he was seen** *of me also, as of one born out of due time.*

Jesus the Christ was born only once; he died only once; he arose only once; BUT he has made himself known literally countless times in the salvation and deliverance of men, women and children, including YOURS, since he rose from the dead more than two thousand years ago. These facts, that is, of the birth, death, burial, resurrection and manifestation of Jesus Christ, evil spirits will not confess.

WE ARE AT WAR

Ephesians 6:11-12. **Our battle is a spiritual one.**
Put on the whole armour of God, that ye may be able to stand against the wiles of the devil. 12 For we wrestle not against flesh and blood, but against principalities, against powers, against the rulers of the darkness of this world, against spiritual wickedness (wicked spirits) *in high places.*

This war we fight is greater than one can imagine. Former (Portland, Oregon) Bible Temple Pastor Dick Iverson has described it this way:

"God is at war with the evil man's spirit and the evil spirits of satanic majesty. Satan and his spirits are at war with man's spirits and the Spirit of God. It is greater than a world war; it is a universal war. This is, in fact, the real battleground of good and evil; right against wrong."

2 Corinthians 10:3-5. **The real battle is in a person's mind.**
For though we walk in the flesh, we do not war after the flesh: 4 (For the weapons of our warfare are not carnal, but mighty through God to the pulling down of strong holds;) 5 Casting down imaginations, and every high thing that exalteth itself against the knowledge of God, and bringing into captivity every thought to the obedience of Christ . . .

You will find that the devil doesn't usually come up to a person and hit him, but he comes in a subtle way to our thought-life and mind. Do you remember this Biblical account from Genesis? *"Now the serpent was more subtil (subtle) than any beast of the field which the LORD God had made."*

This word "subtle" comes from Latin through Old French into our English language and means 'cunning or crafty.' Therefore, enemy

I Would Not Have You Ignorant

spirits can come in to our thought-life and mind in cunning and crafty ways to destroy us. However, the prophet Isaiah encourages us by stating *"We have a strong city; salvation will God appoint for walls and bulwarks . . . Thou wilt keep him in perfect peace, whose mind* (thought, or imagination) *is stayed thee: because he trusteth in thee."* Isaiah 26:3

Thoughts, whether good or bad, are sourced in the spirit. Bodies do not think, but spirits do. J. Dwight Pentecost says, "God and Satan are in a battle for the minds of men. It is the mind that Satan wants, for if he can control the mind, he eventually can control the will."

WHAT IS THE DISCERNING OF SPIRITS?

Three recognized men of God have defined this particular gift of the Holy Spirit:

Kenneth Hagin says that simply speaking, it is a gift that "gives insight into the spirit world."

Dick Iverson is quoted as saying the gift of discerning of spirits is a "God-given ability to recognize the identity of the spirits which are behind different manifestations or activities."

C. Peter Wagner relates that it is "The special ability God gives to some members of the Body of Christ which enables them to know with assurance whether certain behavior purported to be of God is in reality divine, human or satanic."

All mature Christians can discern (distinguish) good from evil, and right from wrong. Hebrews 5:13-14. *For every one that useth milk is unskilful in the word of righteousness: for he is a babe. 14 But strong meat belongeth to them that are of full age, even those who by reason of use have their senses exercised to discern both good and evil.*

But, *" . . . to another* (ie. to some) *discerning of spirits . . . " is given.* Cf. 1 Corinthians 12:10.

This gift is generally given to those in leadership positions in the Body of Christ who guide and guard the people of God.

Acts 20:17, 28-30. The Ephesian elders were warned by Paul (an apostle, church leader). *And from Miletus, he sent to Ephesus and called the elders of the church. 28 Take heed therefore unto yourselves, and to all the flock, over the which the Holy Ghost hath made you overseers, to feed the church of God, which he hath purchased with his own blood. 29 For I know this, that after my departing shall grievous wolves enter in among you, not sparing the flock. 30 Also of your own selves shall men arise, speaking perverse things, to draw away disciples after them.*

Matthew 7:15-16. Wolves in sheep's clothing are known by their fruit. Jesus warned future church leaders. *Beware of false prophets, which come to you in sheep's clothing, but inwardly they are ravening wolves. 16 Ye shall know them by their fruits. Do men gather grapes of thorns, or figs of thistles?*

Ezekiel 33:7-9. Ezekiel (a prophet) was appointed to watch the people. He speaks a word as God reveals the condition of the people's hearts. *So thou, O son of man, I have set thee a watchman unto the house of Israel; therefore thou shalt hear the word at my mouth, and warn them from me. 8 When I say unto the wicked, O wicked man, thou shalt surely die; if thou dost not speak to warn the wicked from his way, that wicked man shall die in his iniquity; but his blood will I require at thine hand. 9 Nevertheless, if thou warn the wicked of his way to turn from it; if he do not turn from his way, he shall die in his iniquity; but thou hast delivered thy soul.*

In his book "The Holy Spirit Today," Pastor-Teacher Dick Iverson suggests that one who is used by the Holy Spirit in this gift may have a special ability to discern areas of human spirits, that is attitudes, needs in people's lives etc., while another may have the ability to discern areas of demonic activity. Yet others may have little discernment in these areas but have an ability to clearly discern which gifts and manifestations are of God and which are not. This variety is much like the gift(s) of healing(s).

Iverson describes that the purpose of this gift is "to protect, guard, guide and properly feed the flock of God."

Hagin relates that "discerning of spirits also implies 'seeing. "By this gift, one can see into the spirit world."

2 Kings 6:13-18. *And he said, Go and spy where he is, that I may send and fetch him. And it was told him, saying, Behold, he is in Dothan. 14 Therefore sent he thither horses, and chariots, and a great host: and they came by night, and compassed the city about. 15 And when the servant of the man of God was risen early, and gone forth, behold, an host compassed the city both with horses and chariots. And his servant said unto him, Alas, my master! how shall we do? 16 And he answered, Fear not: for they that be with us are more than they that be with them. 17 And Elisha prayed, and said, Lord, I pray thee, open his eyes, that he may see. And the Lord opened the eyes of the young man; and he saw: and, behold, the mountain was full of horses and chariots of fire round about Elisha. 18 And when they came down to him, Elisha prayed unto the Lord, and said, Smite this people, I pray thee, with blindness. And he smote them with blindness according to the word of Elisha.*

Discerning spirits in the New Testament

Mark 5:35-42. **Spirit of doubt, unbelief.**
While he yet spake, there came from the ruler of the synagogue's house certain which said, Thy daughter is dead: why troublest thou the Master any further? 36 As soon as Jesus heard the word that was spoken, he saith unto the ruler of the synagogue, Be not afraid, only believe. 37 And he suffered no man to follow him, save Peter, and James, and John the brother of James. 38 And he cometh to the house of the ruler of the synagogue, and seeth the tumult, and them that wept and wailed greatly. 39 And when he was come in, he saith unto them, Why make ye this ado, and weep? the damsel is not dead, but sleepeth. 40 And they laughed him to scorn. But when he had put them all out, he taketh the father and the mother of the damsel, and them that were with him, and entereth in where the damsel was lying. 41 And he took the damsel by the hand, and said unto her, Talitha cumi; which is, being interpreted, Damsel, I say unto thee,

arise. 42 And straightway the damsel arose, and walked; for she was of the age of twelve years. And they were astonished with a great astonishment.

Luke 4:33-37. **Unclean spirit.**
And in the synagogue there was a man, which had a spirit of an unclean devil, and cried out with a loud voice, 34 Saying, Let us alone; what have we to do with thee, thou Jesus of Nazareth? art thou come to destroy us? I know thee who thou art; the Holy One of God. 35 And Jesus rebuked him, saying, Hold thy peace, and come out of him. And when the devil had thrown him in the midst, he came out of him, and hurt him not. 36 And they were all amazed, and spake among themselves, saying, What a word is this! for with authority and power he commandeth the unclean spirits, and they come out. 37 And the fame of him went out into every place of the country round about.

Luke 13:11-13. **Spirit of infirmity.**
And, behold, there was a woman which had a spirit of infirmity eighteen years, and was bowed together, and could in no wise lift up herself. 12 And when Jesus saw her, he called her to him, and said unto her, Woman, thou art loosed from thine infirmity. 13 And he laid his hands on her: and immediately she was made straight, and glorified God.

Acts 16:16-18. **Spirits of divination.**
And it came to pass, as we went to prayer, a certain damsel possessed with a spirit of divination met us, which brought her masters much gain by soothsaying: 17 The same followed Paul and us, and cried, saying, These men are the servants of the most high God, which shew unto us the way of salvation. 18 And this did she many days. But Paul, being grieved, turned and said to the spirit, I command thee in the name of Jesus Christ to come out of her. And he came out the same hour.

Discernment begins with whether or not the manifestation is one of encouragement, joy or fear. The following references clarify this truth.
2 Timothy 1:7. *For God hath not given us the spirit of fear; but of*

power, and of love, and of a sound mind.

1 John 4:18 (The Living Bible). *We need have no fear of someone who loves us perfectly; his perfect love for us eliminates all dread of what he might do to us. If we are afraid, it is for fear of what he might do to us and shows that we are not fully convinced that he really loves us.*

Instances of Jesus discerning spirits.

Matthew 9:1-8 (esp 4). *And he entered into a ship, and passed over, and came into his own city. 2 And, behold, they brought to him a man sick of the palsy, lying on a bed: and Jesus seeing their faith said unto the sick of the palsy; Son, be of good cheer; thy sins be forgiven thee. 3 And, behold, certain of the scribes said within themselves, This man blasphemeth. 4 And Jesus knowing their thoughts said, Wherefore think ye evil in your hearts? 5 For whether is easier, to say, Thy sins be forgiven thee; or to say, Arise, and walk? 6 But that ye may know that the Son of man hath power on earth to forgive sins, (then saith he to the sick of the palsy,) Arise, take up thy bed, and go unto thine house. 7 And he arose, and departed to his house. 8 But when the multitudes saw it, they marvelled, and glorified God, which had given such power unto men.*

Matthew 12:25. Many times this gift is coupled with the Word of Knowledge. *And Jesus knew their thoughts, and said unto them, Every kingdom divided against itself is brought to desolation; and every city or house divided against itself shall not stand:*

Matthew 16:15-17. God-inspired revelation. *He saith unto them, But whom say ye that I am? 16 And Simon Peter answered and said, Thou art the Christ, the Son of the living God. 17 And Jesus answered and said unto him, Blessed art thou, Simon Barjona: for flesh and blood hath not revealed it unto thee, but my Father which is in heaven.*

Matthew 16:21-23. Satan-inspired words. *From that time forth began Jesus to shew unto his disciples, how that he must go unto*

Jerusalem, and suffer many things of the elders and chief priests and scribes, and be killed, and be raised again the third day. 22 Then Peter took him, and began to rebuke him, saying, Be it far from thee, Lord: this shall not be unto thee. 23 But he turned, and said unto Peter, Get thee behind me, Satan: thou art an offence unto me: for thou savourest not the things that be of God, but those that be of men.

Mark 5:5-13. Legion of unclean spirits. *And always, night and day, he was in the mountains, and in the tombs, crying, and cutting himself with stones. 6 But when he saw Jesus afar off, he ran and worshipped him, 7 And cried with a loud voice, and said, What have I to do with thee, Jesus, thou Son of the most high God? I adjure thee by God, that thou torment me not. 8 For he said unto him, Come out of the man, thou unclean spirit. 9 And he asked him, What is thy name? And he answered, saying, My name is Legion: for we are many. 10 And he besought him much that he would not send them away out of the country. 11 Now there was there nigh unto the mountains a great herd of swine feeding. 12 And all the devils besought him, saying, Send us into the swine, that we may enter into them. 13 And forthwith Jesus gave them leave. And the unclean spirits went out, and entered into the swine: and the herd ran violently down a steep place into the sea, (they were about two thousand;) and were choked in the sea.*

Luke 5:22. *But when Jesus perceived their thoughts, he answering said unto them, What reason ye in your hearts?*

New Testament leaders discerned spirits.

Acts 5:1-10. Evil and human spirits discerned. Note bold type references. Ananias and Sapphira had a lying spirit. *But a certain man named Ananias, with Sapphira his wife, sold a possession, 2 And kept back part of the price, his wife also being privy to it, and brought a certain part, and laid it at the apostles' feet. 3 But Peter said, Ananias,* **why hath Satan filled thine heart** *to lie to the Holy Ghost, and to keep back part of the price of the land? 4 Whilst it remained, was it not thine own? and after it was sold, was it not in thine own power?* **why hast thou conceived this thing in thine**

I Would Not Have You Ignorant

heart? thou hast not lied unto men, but unto God. 5 And Ananias hearing these words fell down, and gave up the ghost: and great fear came on all them that heard these things. 6 And the young men arose, wound him up, and carried him out, and buried him. 7 And it was about the space of three hours after, when his wife, not knowing what was done, came in. 8 And Peter answered unto her, Tell me whether ye sold the land for so much? And she said, Yea, for so much. 9 Then Peter said unto her, **How is it that ye have agreed together** *to tempt the Spirit of the Lord? behold, the feet of them which have buried thy husband are at the door, and shall carry thee out. 10 Then fell she down straightway at his feet, and yielded up the ghost: and the young men came in, and found her dead, and, carrying her forth, buried her by her husband.*

Acts 8:9-23. **Simon had a spirit of bitterness.** *But there was a certain man, called Simon, which beforetime in the same city used sorcery, and bewitched the people of Samaria, giving out that himself was some great one: 10 To whom they all gave heed, from the least to the greatest, saying, This man is the great power of God. 11 And to him they had regard, because that of long time he had bewitched them with sorceries. 12 But when they believed Philip preaching the things concerning the kingdom of God, and the name of Jesus Christ, they were baptized, both men and women. 13 Then Simon himself believed also: and when he was baptized, he continued with Philip, and wondered, beholding the miracles and signs which were done. 14 Now when the apostles which were at Jerusalem heard that Samaria had received the word of God, they sent unto them Peter and John: 15 Who, when they were come down, prayed for them, that they might receive the Holy Ghost: 16 (For as yet he was fallen upon none of them: only they were baptized in the name of the Lord Jesus.) 17 Then laid they their hands on them, and they received the Holy Ghost. 18 And when Simon saw that through laying on of the apostles' hands the Holy Ghost was given, he offered them money, 19 Saying, Give me also this power, that on whomsoever I lay hands, he may receive the Holy Ghost. 20 But Peter said unto him, Thy money perish with thee, because thou hast thought that the gift of God may be purchased with money. 21 Thou hast neither part nor lot in this matter: for thy heart is not right in the sight of God. 22 Repent therefore of this thy wickedness, and* *pray God, if perhaps the thought of thine heart may be forgiven thee. 23 For I perceive that thou art in the gall of bitterness, and in the bond of iniquity.*

Acts 13:9-12. **Elymas had a spirit of perversion.** *Then Saul, (who also is called Paul,) filled with the Holy Ghost, set his eyes on him, 10 And said, O full of all subtilty and all mischief, thou child of the devil, thou enemy of all righteousness, wilt thou not cease to pervert the right ways of the Lord? 11 And now, behold, the hand of the Lord is upon thee, and thou shalt be blind, not seeing the sun for a season. And immediately there fell on him a mist and a darkness; and he went about seeking some to lead him by the hand. 12 Then the deputy, when he saw what was done, believed, being astonished at the doctrine of the Lord.*

The gift of discerning of spirits usually operates closely with the other gifts of the word of knowledge, wisdom, faith and possibly even the working of miracles.

The Last Word . . .

This brings this study on the Gifts of the Spirit to an end, but in conclusion, we would like to make special mention of what Pastor Dick Iverson of Portland, Oregon's Bible Temple, now The City Church, says about these Spiritual Gifts.

"These gifts could be called the 'senses of the Church.' Just as man has five senses through which he contacts the world around him, so the church has been given these nine spiritual senses to contact the spiritual world.

These [five] senses are vitally important to human life. One who lacks them is nearly a vegetable. The same is true in the spiritual. The [nine] gifts of the Spirit are just as essential for the growth and protection of the body of Christ as the five senses are to the human body.

A child without his senses will not be able to grow and develop as a normal child. This is the condition of churches which try to grow without the gifts. They can struggle along with 'professional evangelism' and 'professional ministers' and try to compete with the world in theatrical entertainment, etc., but real growth comes as these gifts function in the assemblies. We need never wonder why churches are 'crippled' if these gifts do not function.

A person being used in the gifts of the Holy Spirit should always be in prayer/communion with God, studying and meditating on the Word of God, and building himself up by praying in tongues."

May we learn to give the Holy Spirit time to minister when we gather together. Remember, *"where the Spirit is Lord, there is liberty."* Let's make Him the Lord of our lives and church services. If and when we do, don't you think the place will blow away, just like on the Day of Pentecost when He manifested Himself in a rushing mighty wind?

We hope this book has enabled you to understand more about how the Holy Spirit wants to minister among His church. I think we all want to see and experience more of Him. Therefore let us . . .

Covet earnestly the best gifts. 1 Corinthians 12:31

But all these (gifts) *worketh that one and the selfsame Spirit, dividing to every man severally as He will.* 1 Corinthians 12:11

About the author . . .

Nils married his wife, Andrea in 1976 and left for Japan in January of 1978 as ordained missionaries out of Seattle's old Bethel Temple. They went directly to the southern island of Kyushu where they began learning Japanese and the "ropes" of missionary life under the supervision of leaders of an already established local Japanese church.

After four years, in 1982 they stepped out on their own and began pioneering what is now the Munakata Bethel Christian Center. Munakata City is a "bed town" of 95,000-plus people located between two metropolises (Kita Kyushu City to the north, and Fukuoka City to the south) of over one million each.

The work began in their rented house, and when it became too small, the church moved to a rental facility. After being there for several years, they were asked to move. Nils & Andrea were led to lease a piece of property and build a permanent structure in the city. In 1993 the permanent building was completed, debt free. The property was purchased in January 2017 from its owner and is now in the process of becoming a recognized religious corporation.

The church has developed into an active group of believers being governed by the Holy Spirit and a solid-faith group of elders and deacons, being overseen now by Pastors Jim & Tracy Xavier.

I Would Not Have You Ignorant

In starting from zero, a pioneer work's beginnings are based on "building relationships" with people in the community. This has been one of our most important tools in the work as missionaries. People who have come to the church have found that it is not at all like they thought: quiet, somber and religious, but rather bright, lively, expressive and a place that has the answers to life's problems. Please feel free to view the church web page at: http://www.munakatabethel.com/

Nils majored in Radio-TV communications with an emphasis on TV news casting and had fully intended on following that career. However, in 1973 he was led to enroll in the Bethel Temple Bible School, which was the beginning of seeing the fulfillment of his childhood dream, "I wanna be a missionary when I grow up."

Even though he changed fields, he finds himself doing exactly what he studied in Radio-TV news casting so many years ago. Besides weekly preaching and teaching for over thirty years, he continues to be actively involved in performing wedding ceremonies for many, many Japanese couples who desire to be married in the atmosphere of a genuine Christian church by a genuine pastor.

Even though Nils & Andrea have been in active ministry for over thirty years, Nils says they still don't know it all. "We're still learning," he says, "we'll be learning until we die. Life is like being in school, it's full of tests. We won't graduate until the day we breathe our last. But, until then we'll give it our best shot because we love our Principal!"

Profile Timeline: Nils Olson

June 1966 — Graduated Lakes High School, Tacoma, WA.
1966-1969 — Tacoma Community College (Mass Media).
1971-1973—Clover Park Vocational-Technical Institute, Tacoma, WA (Graduated, Radio-TV news).
1974-1977—Bethel Temple Bible School. Graduated.
[Nils met Andrea here where she was also a student.]
July 1977—Ordination, Bethel Temple's Mirror Lake Campground, Federal Way, WA. Both Nils & Andrea carry credential cards from Bethel Fellowship International.
January 1978 — Arrived in Japan.
1978-1982—Internship at Kurume Bethel Christ Church.
1982—Munakata Bethel Christian Center (MBCC) established.
1982-November, 2016—Pastored MBCC. Now retired and serving as senior missionaries, Nils and his wife, Andrea live in Munakata City.

Nils has also written a collection of personal anecdotes, stories, memories and thoughts in his book titled

"My Chapter of the Story" available from:

www.createspace.com/3996295.

Sketch by artist GAHO Yasuoka of ANO Planning, Fukuoka, Japan.

Cover design by James Xavier.

I Would Not Have You Ignorant

*But this is that which was spoken by the prophet Joel . . .
And it shall come to pass in the last days, saith God,*
I will pour out of my Spirit upon all flesh . . .

Made in the USA
San Bernardino, CA
07 July 2017